R0061405858

01/2012

W9-AMO-134

Return to
SAWYERTON SPRINGS

To learn more about Andy Andrews,
or to book him for your next speaking event,
visit: **www.AndyAndrews.com**

OTHER BOOKS BY ANDY ANDREWS

The Traveler's Gift

The Lost Choice

Island of Saints

The Noticer

Socks for Christmas

The Butterfly Effect

Return to
SAWYERTON SPRINGS

A *Mostly* TRUE TALE FILLED WITH
LOVE, LEARNING, *and* LAUGHTER

ANDY ANDREWS

Hansen House
Newport Beach, CA

Published by Hansen House, Inc., Newport Beach, California · (949) 764-2640

Cataloging Information available from the Library of Congress

ISBN: 978-0-9819709-1-2

12 11 10 09   4 3 2 1
1st edition, September 2009

Printed in the United States of America

CONTACT ANDY

To book Andy for corporate events, call:

(800) 726-ANDY (2639)

For more information, go to:

www.AndyAndrews.com

Dedicated to Kevin and Glenda Perkins.

*To remain best friends from childhood,
through high school, college, and adulthood
is a rare thing indeed.*

I am honored to know you.

AUTHOR'S NOTE

THROUGH THE YEARS, I HAVE BEEN DESCRIBED BY FRIENDS and family as an optimist and a pessimist. I have been labeled focused *and* disorganized. Once, my wife publicly praised my ability to compromise on the same day she later criticized me for having a stubborn nature.

Here and now, I confess that it is all true. I am calm *and* hot-headed, observant *and* oblivious, a master of my emotions *and* a blubbering mess. I am a man who has reached this point in my life without medication or incarceration. I consider myself normal in every sense of the word. I am neither a great success nor a slovenly failure. I am happy except when I am sad, energetic except when I am tired, and patient with my children . . . except when I am not.

In what many call the "middle-aged years" of my life, I have become comfortable with the idea that I am a walking contradiction. On occasion, I am even proud of the fact. But there is no doubt in my mind that my hometown is to blame. "They" made me what I am. And I am not alone!

Amazing, isn't it? Our hometowns have sent us into the world with mispronunciations, odd habits, and predetermined beliefs about ourselves and each other. And we have stories—stories we tell and retell about the people with whom the fabric of our lives was inexorably woven.

Sawyerton Springs, Alabama, is such a place. It is more memory to me now than geographic location, though I occasionally visit to catch up on the kind of news that never seems to make it to Yahoo or MSN. Who died, who got married, what happened at the wedding that you will not believe . . . those kinds of things.

The town is not famous. In fact, it is missing from several state maps. There is nothing there that is the biggest or the best or the first of anything. There is, on second thought, a *last* distinction held by Sawyerton Springs . . .

Myra Fletcher had lived her entire sixty-eight years at the home in which she was born just outside of town. The two-acre lot bordered a wooded area where an artillery battle had been fought during the civil war. A point of pride for the Fletcher family had long been the cannonball stuck high up in an old oak tree where it could be plainly seen. Over time, a limb had grown from the spot, making the large sphere more and more visible.

It was a blustery March morning when the cannonball finally fell. Myra (everyone assumed when they found her) had been raking leaves under the oak when she was fatally struck on the head by what was later determined to be a twelve-pound ball of iron. It wasn't until the funeral two days later that everyone realized that Myra Regina Fletcher had become the last official casualty of the Civil War . . . in 1974.

I grew up in Sawyerton Springs. I have somehow repressed much of what happened during those years and have rarely, if ever, related these memories. Why, I do not know. I hope it is not embarrassment, though if I were entirely honest that might be a factor. No one can bring down a cloud of mortification like those who know us best.

And they do know me there. This was the place I learned to shake hands with a firm grip and "look a person in the eye when you do it." Someone in this small town that raised me to be the man I now am remembers my first laugh, my first cry, and my first curse word. Of course, as one might expect, those memories are held over me, dangled occasionally for public consumption by the local keepers of humility.

The very week one of my books first hit the *New York Times* bestsellers list, I was reminded by the mayor—from the podium at the Rotary Club luncheon—about the time Billy Pat Williams put down the word "suit" in the Rotarian Scrabble Tournament and I immediately jumped up and yelled, "Su it? What kind of word is su it?"

The message was clear . . . you're not any smarter than the rest of us.

Smart or not, as an author who is no longer "under the gun" or tied to a particular genre, I have taken a year to complete this written documentation of my hometown. I have included the community's current activities in addition to my recollections of its past. Don't expect this to be a complete or thorough history of my childhood or of Sawyerton Springs itself as I was determined to leave out the boring parts.

And I did.

Andy Andrews
Orange Beach, Alabama

SUMMER

CHAPTER 1

IN A TOWN WITHOUT A MOVIE THEATER OR FAST FOOD restaurant, life is divided into three distinct seasons: football, basketball, and baseball. Weeks, months, and, yes, time itself revolves around the children, their practices and games. Most kids played all three sports, but at eleven years of age, I didn't weigh enough to play football and measurements for basketball had me at a lofty four feet five inches. It was baseball for me and had been for several years. This year, however, I was going to be a "starter" at second base.

As we milled around, one could easily pick out the kids from last year's team: Lee Peyton, Kevin Perkins, Steve Krotzer, Phillip Wilson, Charles Raymond Floyd, and, of course, me. We all had on last year's hats. They were off-white with a dark-blue bill and a big "FNB" on the front. First National Bank, our sponsor, would be giving everyone new hats—we knew that. But in the meantime, we wanted to be sure that our new coach could tell the veterans from the rookies.

None of us had met our new coach. His name was Mr. Simpson. He was, we were told, "new to the area." "New to the area" and "new in town" were two different things. If someone was new in town, that generally meant that he had moved from someplace we had heard of and was probably still within driving distance of his cousins. New to the area, however, was a hint that this person was "from the North."

Living as we did, in the southern part of Alabama, "North" to me was Birmingham. At the time, I suppose I was somewhat suspicious of people from the North. To be certain, it was a tiny distinction, yet the phrase brought visions of Vikings and pillaging to my mind. This created an intense curiosity about Mr. Simpson—almost a feeling of danger. After all, I had been told more than once that these people could be nice, but they were different. The word "different" was always articulated with a pause before it and with eyebrows raised.

Mr. Simpson parked his station wagon and gathered the equipment from the back. Bats, balls, catcher's gear. Yep, it was all there. We were watching him from the backstop as if he were some wild animal at the zoo. We noticed a boy with him. The boy had red hair and more freckles than I had seen on any human since my Aunt Nancy Jane (and she had freckles on her fingernails!). The boy, we figured, was the coach's son, since Mr. Simpson also had red hair and more than his share of freckles.

"Hi, boys," Mr. Simpson said as he dumped the equipment near home plate. "My name is Hankin Simpson, and I'm your new coach."

I glanced to my right. Kevin Perkins was smirking and looking at me. Kevin was kind of a smart aleck, and I knew what he was thinking: *Hankin? Where did he come from?*

Placing his hand on the shoulder of the red-headed boy, Mr. Simpson continued. "I want you to meet my son. This is Hankin, Jr."

I didn't dare look toward Kevin. I didn't need to. I could feel him smirking from where I was.

"Now boys," the coach continued, "I'm new to the area."

Well, I thought, *that explains "Hankin"* . . .

"But I'm sure," he said, "that it's going to be a great season. Okay? Okay! Now before we begin practice, everybody take a rap!"

And with that, he clapped his hands and busied himself arranging the equipment.

We shuffled our feet and looked at each other. *What*, we wondered, *did he want us to do? Take a what? A rap? What was a rap?*

Hankin, Jr., we saw, had begun to trot around the field, and figuring that he knew what he was doing, we trotted after him.

"Rap is a Northern word," whispered Phillip as we jogged along. "It means 'to run'."

I wasn't sure whether to believe him or not. Kevin was a smart aleck, but Phillip Wilson made things up. He was what five-year-olds called a storyteller, what we called a fibber, and what adults called a liar. He could look you right in the eye, tell you a fib so convincingly that you never doubted a word he said. Even though I had never trusted him, I kept him as a friend because I had heard my dad tell my mom that Phillip was certain to become president one day.

Back at home plate, all out of breath from running a rap, we gathered around Mr. Simpson, quite sure that he would now assign positions. We veterans thrust our caps toward his face, a virtual sea of FNBs, silently pleading with the man not to look at one of us and say, "Right field."

Since time began, all Little Leaguers have instinctively feared right field. There are nine positions on a baseball diamond, and in the glamour department, right field ranks dead last. Most batters are right-handed and will hit the ball to leftfield; therefore, a coach who desires to avoid long losing streaks will naturally place his weakest player in right.

I'd had my brush with this humiliation two years earlier as the weak link for Henley's Hardware (green hat, white "H"). Standing in right field game after game with nary a ball hit my way, I never believed the adults who told me I was an integral part of the team. I couldn't catch, but I wasn't stupid. A permanent residence in right field was an embarrassment. It was a curse. I was certain that I had been branded for the rest of my life. I could imagine myself as a grownup going to a job interview and being told, "We're sorry, there's no place for you at NASA. We see on your record that you played right field."

"Boys," Mr. Simpson began, "we're gonna be a winner this year. I'm excited about this team. Before we really get going, I want to check you out at certain positions. Don't worry if you're new to the game. On my team, everyone gets to pray."

Excuse me? Did he say "pray"? I looked at Steve Krotzer. He was jabbing Charles Raymond Floyd in the ribs. Lee Peyton was jabbing Kevin, and Phillip jabbed me.

"I know this is just practice," the coach continued, "but no matter . . . I want you to pray your hearts out!"

This team, I thought, *is in trouble.* Either someone had told our new leader that last year we lost seventeen out of twenty-three games, or he took one look at us and decided that we were a bunch of rejects. What it boiled down to, I was beginning to believe, was that if we were to have any chance of a winning season, Mr. Simpson had settled on prayer as our only hope.

Thirty minutes later we were in the positions that would be ours, more or less, for the rest of the year. I was at second base, so I was happy. Steve was at first, Kevin at third, Lee was our catcher, and Charles Raymond stood in right field with the other kids who couldn't catch.

Phillip Wilson, meanwhile, pouted at shortstop. He wanted to pitch. Actually, we wanted him to pitch too, but as soon as we had seen that there was a Hankin Simpson, Jr., we knew that he would not. Every member of First National Bank was acutely aware of that age-old Little League Law: If the coach has a son, the team has a pitcher.

This has become such an accepted part of coaching methodology that it is no longer questioned. A Little League coach is usually the father of one of the players, and he always has a blind spot where his child is concerned. Can the kid throw strikes? Has he got a curve ball? Does he trip over his own feet? None of that really matters— he's the coach's son. Put him on the mound. He's a pitcher.

We practiced hard that first day. Trying to show Mr. Simpson our "stuff," we dove for grounders, swung for the fence, and generally showed as much hustle as we could muster. We didn't seem to be a vastly improved team from the year before. I blew a sure double play, our pitcher threw the ball over the backstop, and Charles Raymond got hit in the head by a pop fly and cried.

Coach Simpson didn't say much, but when he did, he was still saying things we didn't understand: "Take another rap. Pray hard! Pray hard!" We were a confused group of kids. It was at the end of practice, however, during the compulsory pep talk, when everything became crystal clear.

"There is one thing about this game you can count on," he said. "If you do not rearn to watch the basebarr hit the basebarr grove, you wirr never be an excerrent basebarr prayer."

Well, we were stunned. After two and a half hours of total darkness, we suddenly understood. A rap? Pray? He had wanted us to take a *lap*! He had wanted us to *play* hard! How could we have been so blind?

From the depths of a pep talk to which no one was listening—like a bolt from the blue—those weird words all came together and made sense. Certain words from his last sentence jumped out at us like sparks from a bonfire. "Blah blah blah rearn blah blah blah basebarr blah blah basebarr grove, blah blah wirr blah blah excerrent basebarr prayer!"

It was now an undeniable fact that had become apparent to us all in one fell swoop. Coach Simpson could not say his *l*'s!

We stood, silently exchanging furtive glances as Hankin, Junior and Senior, got in their car and drove away. No one had spoken a word yet, but we all suspected that we had been the recipients of a miracle from God. We could scarcely contain our collective excitement. To a group of eleven-year-old boys, nothing beats having a human target at which to laugh. Double the fun if the boys are able to mimic the target, and triple if the unfortunate target happens to be an adult!

Kevin was smirking again. We shuffled around and snickered a bit. Then, it started.

Charles Raymond: "I'm a basebarr prayer."

Steve: "No you ain't. You're a right fierder!"

Kevin: "Take a rap! Take a rap!"

Phillip: "Did you hear him call me 'Phirrip'?"

Lee: "Coach Simpson? I rike him. I rearry do!"

And so it continued until we were exhausted. Finally able to breathe at last, we lounged in the dirt around home plate. Phillip spoke first, this time seriously. "I think he's oriental," he said. Oriental people use the letter *r* in the place of the letter *l* when they speak English, because they don't have the letter *l* in their own language. That's why he does it. Coach Simpson is oriental. Remember? He said he was new to the area . . . he's oriental."

"Oriental?" Charles Raymond asked. "Is that like when you don't know your way around?"

Kevin smirked. "No, Stupe," he said. "He means Japanese, right?"

Kevin glanced my way. I wanted to tell Phillip that I had never seen a six-foot-three-inch, 240-pound, red-haired, freckled-faced Japanese guy before. That's what I wanted to say, but Phillip was looking at me with such an air of self-confidence that I knew the truth did not stand a chance against such a convincing opponent.

I was about to give it a try anyway when Lee suddenly giggled. "What?" we demanded.

"I was just thinking . . ." Lee said as he tried to talk through his laughter. "I was just thinking that this year sometime, I'm gonna be rounding third . . ."

He stopped and laughed. "I'm gonna be rounding third headed toward this here home plate and . . ." He was really laughing now.

"Tell us," we urged.

"I'm gonna be headed toward this here home plate, and Coach Simpson's gonna yell, 'Sride, Ree! Sride!'"

We never mentioned the Oriental Theory again. Kevin told me privately one day that he thought Phillip was "full of mess." I took that to be Kevin's way of saying that he didn't believe Coach Simpson was Japanese either. Not that it would have mattered. One of our best friends, Peter Chin, was Japanese or something. And he said his *l*'s perfectly, except, of course, when he was mimicking Coach Simpson with us.

Several memories of that year still remain clear in my mind. To this day, Phillip Wilson is "Phirrip" to everyone who played on that team. And no one has forgotten the game that Lee Peyton rounded third, headed for home, and fell down before he got there, laughing, because Coach Simpson really did yell, "Sride, Ree! Sride!"

If I had to choose one capsule of time during that season to carry with me for the rest of my life, it would have to be the day Steve Krotzer got kicked off the team. Maybe kicked off is too harsh. Actually, he was transferred to another team because the league president found out that Steve's family was living in another district.

It was a messy situation. Steve had played with us for four years. Two years on Henley's Hardware and two with First National Bank. Now they were sending him to play with the team—Sand Dollar Shoes—near his home. We were sick. Steve was our friend and a darn good first baseman. He didn't want to go. We didn't want him to leave. But that last day did arrive.

When practice was over, Coach Simpson gathered us around the pitcher's mound. He had his hand on Steve's shoulder. "Boys," he began, "this is a sad day. We're going to miss Steve. He's a fine barrprayer and a fine young man."

Steve was close to tears. We were too.

"I don't understand the inner workings of the system," Coach Simpson continued, "and I'm not sure why this has happened. But I do know one thing . . . and rook at me when I say this, because this is important. I want everyone of you to know . . . that this was not Steve's faurt."

As a group, Steve included, we jumped as if ten thousand volts of electricity had passed through our bodies. Did he say what we thought he said? Surely not.

"No," he went on, "this was not Steve's faurt, and it wasn't my faurt."

Yes, he most definitely, absolutely said what we thought he said! Oh sure, we knew what he meant; we'd been unconsciously translating Simpsonisms all year. He was telling us that it wasn't Steve's "fault" . . . but that wasn't what we were hearing!

"It wasn't Steve's parent's faurt either. I guess, really, it was nobody's faurt."

It was too good to be true. Of all the words in the world guaranteed to make eleven-year-old boys laugh, only one of them is all by itself at the top of the list. And our coach—an adult—was saying that word over and over and over.

"If it's anyone's faurt, it's the system's faurt. So don't pin the faurt on any one person, because it is just not their faurt!"

Well, I am not exaggerating when I say that we were literally rolling on the ground. We were crying. Coach Simpson thought we really were crying and became concerned. He sounded desperate as he tried to comfort us, but the more he explained that it wasn't our "faurt," the more out of hand things became.

Soon tears were rolling down Coach Simpson's face too. Several of us felt badly about that later, but as Kevin pointed out, "Hey, don't worry about it. It ain't our faurt!"

* * * * *

I haven't seen Coach Simpson in years. Kevin Perkins and Steve Krotzer were in my wedding. Lee Peyton went to medical school and returned to practice in our town. Charles Raymond Floyd was a late bloomer. He was a center fielder in college, made second-team All American, and played three years of minor league ball. I've totally lost track of Phillip Wilson. The last I heard, he was a used car salesman and perpetually campaigning for mayor in a small town in Louisiana.

Kevin, incidentally, is still my best friend, though he continues to live in Sawyerton Springs, and I have long since moved away. I still remember us all as we were that summer. I can close my eyes and hear the explosions of laughter as we react to something that was, to us, the funniest thing in the world. And I feel a little sad when I think that when we were eleven years old, we may have laughed harder than we ever would again.

CHAPTER 2

HOWARD AND SONYA PEEL EXITED THE INTERSTATE AND immediately heard a thump under the hood of their Mercedes. They looked at each other. Howard shrugged and continued talking. "Anyway, we're almost there, so we might as well get off the main road and see a little bit of the country." They heard another thump.

Sonya glanced sideways at her husband. "Is something wrong with the car?" she asked. "Maybe we should go back to that service station at the exit."

"Nah," Howard answered. "We're fine. It's probably just bad gas. It'll work itself out."

Thirty minutes later, Sonya said, "Nah, we're fine. It's probably just bad gas. It'll work itself out." They were walking at the time.

The Peels are from Chicago. Howard worked as an account executive for a Fortune 500 company while Sonya had raised the kids. They were both in their fifties now, and their children were grown.

For the last twenty years or so, Howard and Sonya had taken their family to the Gulf Coast every June. This, however, was the first time they had gone alone.

Howard wanted it to be a special trip. He had certainly provided his wife with luxuries. She drove a Mercedes and shopped at the finest stores in Chicago, but he felt Sonya needed some spontaneity in her life. And that is why he had decided to get off the interstate.

"Would you mind telling me why you got off the interstate?" Sonya asked as she hobbled down the road in high heels. "I mean, here we are, in the middle of southeast God knows where—walking into God *only* knows what kind of situation. Do you realize that something has happened on every trip we have taken in the last twenty years? At least we're not lost. Most of the time we're lost, and it's always because you won't ask for directions. But at least we're not lost. I remember the time . . ."

As Sonya babbled on, venting her anger, Howard thought about what she was saying. *She's right,* he mused. *At least about me not asking directions. Why won't I do that?* He suspected it was a "man" thing. He couldn't ever remember asking for directions.

Howard tuned her back in. *What was she saying?* he thought. *Oh, the bathroom deal again.* Sonya was now talking about how Howard had not stopped at a rest area an hour ago. She had needed to go then, and now she was mad about it. Howard guessed that was another "man" thing. He would never stop if he had a choice. It was a waste of time. He had a schedule.

"Here comes a car," Howard said, raising his eyebrows.

They turned and faced the car, which was obviously intending to stop anyway. As it pulled onto the grass, Mike Martin rolled down the window. "You folks need a lift, I bet," Mike said. "I saw your car a couple of miles back. Hop in."

"Where are you headed?" Howard asked. He was not about to trust just anyone. He was from the city. He had better sense than that.

"I'm going home," Mike answered. "Be more than happy to give you a ride into town. By the way, my name is Mike Martin."

"What is the next town?" Sonya asked.

Mike was getting a little impatient. He knew from their accent that they were not from Foley or anywhere close, but they sure did seem distrustful. "Sawyerton Springs, ma'am. It's only six and a half miles up the road. 'Course, if you'd rather walk . . ."

"No, no," they said and scrambled into the car. Sonya sat in the front, Howard in the back. He wanted to keep an eye on Mike. *He seems like a nice enough guy,* Howard thought, *but you never know—he might have a body in the trunk.*

"So, Mike, what do you do for a living?" Howard asked.

"I'm a mortician," Mike answered, and he hit the gas.

Entering town, Sonya noticed the welcome sign: Sawyerton Springs . . . A Town You Will Like. Sonya wasn't so sure. Mike had already told them that they were stuck at least until tomorrow morning, but Howard refused to accept it. He insisted that they stop at a service station, so Mike pulled into Dick Rollins's place—it was the only one in town.

"Hey, Dick," Mike said as they drove up, "I'm surprised you're here."

"I'm not," Dick said, smiling. "I just ran by to get my pistol. I'm the starter for the kids' races today."

Mike turned to the Peels. "The town has a picnic every year to kick off the summer," he explained. "It's out by Beauman's Pond. We do sack races and stuff."

Howard nodded, then spoke to Dick. "Mr. uh . . . Rollins', is it? I'm Howard Peel from Chicago. This is my wife, Sonya. We are on our way to the coast. Our car has broken down out on County Road 10, and we really need to get it worked on."

"Love to help you," Dick said, "sure would, but I've got to be at the picnic in twenty minutes."

Howard bit his lip. "Is there anyone else here in town who can fix the car?"

"Yeah," Dick answered. "Joe Bullard could do it in a heartbeat. Roger Luker—he's kind of our cop—he could do it. Kevin Perkins, Rick Carper, Tom Henley . . . all them guys know cars. Miss Luna Myers could probably handle the job. She works on her own car, you know."

"Great," Howard said to Mike. "Let's find one of those people."

"Well . . . I know where to find 'em," Mike said, "but it won't do you any good."

"Why is that?" Howard demanded.

"They're at the picnic." Mike said this as if it were something Howard should have figured out for himself. "Look, we have a nice hotel about two blocks away. Why don't you let me run you over there, you can get checked in and freshened up, then you two can join us at the picnic. If this was an emergency, it'd be different."

Howard's face was blood red. "This is an emergency!" he yelled.

"Is anybody dyin'?" Dick asked.

"No," Howard said grudgingly.

"Then it *ain't* no emergency," Dick replied. "I'll see you at the picnic."

The Vine and Olive Hotel on Main Street is really just a big old house, but Tony and Kristy Hamilton had turned it into a ten-room bed and breakfast back in 1964. It was a two-story wooden structure painted white, and it had green shutters. The huge wrap-around porch was lined with rocking chairs.

Kristy said, "We won't be serving supper tonight. Everybody's eating at the picnic, but don't worry, there'll be plenty for you. Breakfast tomorrow morning at seven-thirty sharp. Here's your key—Room 2. That'll be twenty-four dollars in advance."

As they entered the room, Howard was relieved to see it did have its own bathroom. *If it hadn't*, he thought, *I'd never turn my back on Sonya again.*

"So what do we do now?" he asked.

"The first thing I'm doing is taking off these shoes," Sonya said. "My feet are killing me. Did you notice there's no television?"

"But there is a bathroom," Howard pointed out.

There was a knock on the door. It was Tony. "Do ya'll want to ride over to the picnic with us?" he asked. "We have a horse and buggy we hook up for things like this. Come on, you'll love it. There's nothing to do here."

Seeing Tony's point immediately, Howard and Sonya decided

to take him up on the offer. It was the first time either of them had ever ridden in a buggy, and to Sonya's surprise, she actually enjoyed it. "What's your horse's name?" she asked Kristy.

"Governor," she said. "We named him that because of the resemblance between the part of the horse you are watching now and the face of the guy holding the office." They all laughed.

Sonya found herself enjoying Kristy's company. At the picnic, Kristy introduced her to several of the ladies, including Foncie Bullard, who Sonya said looked familiar. After only a few minutes of talking, they realized that a friend of Sonya's in Chicago had a picture of Foncie in her living room. She was one of Foncie's best friends from Tulane.

Howard helped Tony with the buggy rides. While Tony made trips around the pond, Howard talked with the other men and watched the children play. "I've never been to a place like this," Howard said to Mike. "How long have you lived here?"

"All my life," Mike answered.

"Do you ever want to leave?"

"Sometimes, but only for a week or two. Our friends are here, the school is good, the air is clean . . . and people look out for each other."

Howard turned and looked to where Sonya was sitting on a quilt with Kristy. They seemed to be old friends. His wife was actually howling with laughter. He hadn't seen Sonya that happy in a long time.

"You know, Mike," he said, "I'm embarrassed to say this, but I always thought of you guys down in this part of the country as sort of dull or slow, but you're not."

"No," Mike said, grinning, "and ya'll up your way probably aren't all jerks either."

Just then Dick walked up. "Hey, Howard. Hey, Mike," he greeted the men. "Howard, I got through with the last race and towed your car in. I already got it fixed. Wasn't nothing but a hose to the fuel pump. You're ready to go, Bud!"

Howard frowned. "Dick, I want you to do me a favor. I've never been here, but for some reason, I feel like I'm where I belong, at least for now anyway. All of a sudden I don't want to go to the beach. I'll pay you fifty dollars extra not to tell my wife that the car is fixed."

Dick smiled. "Well, I'm not charging you for the repairs," he said. "I felt bad about keeping you around here longer than you wanted in the first place. But as for telling your wife about the car, I'm sorry, but I already did."

Howard's face fell.

"But if your intention is to stick around," Dick continued, "I don't think you have a problem. Your wife tried to give me a hundred not to tell you!"

CHAPTER 3

"YOU REMIND ME SO MUCH OF YOUR FATHER." I HEAR THAT a lot from the people in town every time I go home. It is a compliment. Though appearance is a factor, I believe it to be the similarity in our personalities to which they are referring. My dad was a nut. Not a professional nut like I have become, but a nut nonetheless.

As I was growing up, he was the pastor, minister of music, and youth director at Grace Fellowship Baptist Church. My friends loved him. They had no choice—he made them laugh! Coming home from a date on any Friday night, I might find twenty kids at our house. They would all be gathered around my dad—all listening to him talk.

"I was a good student," he'd say. "I graduated from the seminary Magna Kum Bah Yah." Everyone would laugh, my mother would roll her eyes, and Dad would be on to something else.

"Speak French, Mr. Andrews," someone would say. He would do it.

"Russian!"

"Spanish!"

He "spoke" them too. My father had never actually learned a foreign language but he had a way of pronouncing individual syllables that seemed incredibly real. Using facial expressions and hand motions, he could convey his crazy thoughts—though no one ever understood a word. To my friends, it was the funniest thing in the world.

Miss Edna Thigpen of the *Sawyerton Springs Sentinel* once asked to interview Dad during what he termed an unusually slow news week even for Sawyerton Springs. When word got out about the upcoming feature, the whole town was in a frenzy of anticipation. Everyone knew that "Brother Andrews" wasn't very tolerant of people who couldn't take a joke, and as he had stated on several occasions, "Miss Edna must've had her sense of humor removed as a child."

No one was disappointed with the article. It included Miss Edna's comments about how lucky the Baptists were to have a pastor who not only spoke fourteen languages, including Swahili, but also to receive guidance from a man who often fished with Billy Graham! I have wondered many times if Dad ever asked forgiveness for those lies. I doubt it.

I was proud of the fact that even the "non-churchgoers" considered my father an okay guy. He was the best Ping-Pong player in town and an above-average third baseman on the Grace Fellowship softball team.

Dad didn't take hypocrisy lightly, and for a minister, he could be extremely direct. Early in his career, he spoke to a group of women who made up the Women's Missionary Union (WMU), one of the most vocal (and volatile) forces a Baptist church ever generated. As local legend has it, he said, "Ladies, I have three things to tell you. Number one is that there are a lot of lost people in this world. Secondly, most of you don't give a damn about them. And thirdly," he added, noting the shock on their faces, "it is a shame that you care more about your pastor having said the word 'damn' than you do about all those lost people!"

My father also had different methods of parenting. While growing up, I received the usual number of spankings and lectures.

The spankings ended when I was about twelve, and although the lectures continued well into my teens, Dad often employed other disciplinary techniques.

One late June afternoon when I was about thirteen, Lee Peyton, Kevin Perkins, and I slipped down to the pond behind our house. Anxious to try out the corncob pipes we'd made the week before, we puffed the tobacco for about twenty minutes and promised each other never to smoke again. After tossing all the evidence into the water, we ate a package of breath mints and forgot the whole episode.

Several days later, Lee and Kevin were at my house watching television. Dad came into the room and sat down for a few minutes. Then, as he left, he tossed us a small photo album and said, "Hey, take a look at the new pictures I just developed."

We shrugged our shoulders and began thumbing through them. It was the usual family stuff. Our dog, my mother and her azalea bush, my sister's birthday party, some kids smoking beside a pond. What! We looked closer. Oh my gosh! That was us! But how?

Well, it didn't take a genius to figure out what he had done, and we were not geniuses. My father had crept through the woods, eased down to the pond, and from behind a tree, had taken a perfectly focused (suitable for framing) picture of us and the cloud of smoke around our heads. He never said another word about the incident, but the message was clear. I wasn't getting away with anything!

And believe me, I rarely tried. Dad wasn't all fun and games. He had certain rules that were unbreakable. "Unbreakable," he would say, "unless you want to be broken!" He was only kidding (I think).

Number One: "You will stand when a lady walks into the room. This includes your sister and your mother."

Dad was sure that my wife would appreciate him for that rule one day. He was right.

Number Two: "You will eat some of everything that is being served. You will eat everything on your plate." Dad, having been born during the Depression, was big on this one, but I was such a picky eater that this rule was no longer in effect by the time my sister arrived. I think "the big liver standoff of 1965" must have worn him down.

Number Three: "Do not hit your sister." This was (no contest) the hardest rule to obey. My sister never had a "do not hit your brother" rule, and subsequently she did so quite often.

Number Four: "Never play in the living room with firecrackers, water balloons, mud, skates, a yo-yo, a bullwhip, or the dog." This rule actually started out as plain old "never play in the living room." All the other things were added one at a time.

Number Five: "Always tell the truth. Half the truth is a lie." My father believed that the truth was like a wild animal—just let it loose and it will defend itself. "It doesn't matter if a thousand people believe something stupid and untrue," he once told me, "it is still stupid and untrue."

On most Sunday mornings, my father walked to church. He said it was to clear his mind and make final edits in his sermon. By 11 o'clock, every pew would be packed with people waiting to hear "what Brother Andrews has come up with this week." For the most part, the congregation enjoyed his message, but he had his detractors too.

Some thought Dad was irreverent—that he was not respectful enough. Once, a visiting preacher concluded his sermon by yelling to everyone that all the televisions should be thrown into the river, all the stereos and radios should be thrown into the river, and all the miniskirts and bikinis should be thrown into the river. When he finally sat down, Dad approached the pulpit and said, "Please rise and join me now in singing hymn number 481, "Shall We Gather at the River."

He once urged his flock not to tell the Methodists that to get into heaven they would need to be carrying a covered dish! These were the kinds of things that made people love my dad. He was convinced that God knew how to smile.

I'll never forget a conversation with my father that occurred shortly after I had gotten my driver's license. I had asked him for the keys to the car and he replied, "I'll let you use the car when you cut your hair."

Thinking I had him cornered, I said, "But, Dad, Jesus had long hair."

"Yes," my father agreed, "he did." Then with a smile, he added, "He also walked everywhere he went."

My dad. He had grown up in the South during the forties and fifties—a product of that place and those times but without many of its prevailing attitudes. He drove to Birmingham to eat publicly with several African-American pastors after the church bombing in 1963.

He didn't have the means to pay for my college, but he saw that I went. He made sure that I worked and paid for it myself. And when I left school to become a "speaker or a comedian or a writer or something," he and my mom were the only people who didn't publicly declare that I had lost my mind. "Son, I am behind you," my father said. "The measure of a person's worth is not in what he does—it's in what he is becoming. I don't care if you want to dig ditches for a living . . . just dig good ones! Then I'll bring my friends around and show 'em the ditches my boy dug. I am proud of you now. But I am prouder of what you are becoming."

Sometimes I watch my children sleep at night and say a prayer for their future. I always include one for their father's part in it. As the nightlight casts shadows over their sweet faces, I think about how proud I am of what they are becoming. And I whisper quietly to them—in awe of the feeling that comes over me: *You remind me so much of my daddy.*

CHAPTER 4

SUMMER WAS A TIME OF INTENSE FREEDOM WHEN I WAS A boy. School was out and my normally attentive parents seemed to relax as completely as I did. We played hard all day with only the instruction to "be home when the streetlights come on." And we always were. A few times, however, we went back out . . .

The tomato was in my hand. I stared at the gleaming white front porch of the Vine and Olive Hotel. There was no one stirring in the small, ten-room bed and breakfast. It was well after midnight, but the light over the front door reached almost to the shadows where I lurked with Brian, my older and much wiser cousin. Brian held an egg.

"Well," he demanded, "you gonna throw it or not?"

Actually, I wasn't sure. I was usually a good kid. I went to church, made almost all Bs in school, and didn't cuss much except for words like *dang* and *durn*. I visited my Aunt Ruth in the nursing home every Thursday afternoon with my mother, and I even let her kiss me on the cheek. Aunt Ruth usually had a brown dribble of snuff juice rolling down her chin.

I was a good kid. Yet here I was running the streets at night with an overripe Better Boy, sizing up the freshly painted porch of one of my father's best friends.

What am I doing? I thought. Mr. and Mrs. Hamilton, the owners of the Vine and Olive, had that very afternoon brought a plate of brownies by our house. My arms slumped to my side. I just couldn't go through with it.

"No guts, no glory," Brian said, smirking.

I threw it. The tomato landed with a "whump" against the front door and splattered a large area of the still-sticky paint on the porch. Almost immediately, a light came on in an upstairs window. Brian, naturally, never threw the egg.

As we ran down the alley beside Henley's Hardware, I was confused. I had not wanted to slip out of my bedroom window an hour earlier. I had not wanted to steal a tomato from the Carper's garden and had not wanted to throw it at the Vine and Olive. In fact, I had decided not to . . . but I had done it anyway!

It must've been the "no guts, no glory" comment. Even though I was not certain what glory awaited a vegetable-throwing eleven-year-old, the statement had offered the opportunity to prove I had guts. *I have guts*, I said to myself. *No brains, maybe, but I do have guts.*

Brian was twelve. Every July, he spent a few days with my family in Sawyerton Springs. His mom, my mother's sister, would put him on a bus from Birmingham with a day's supply of Cheetos, ten or twelve comic books, and a big sign around his neck that said BRIAN.

Brian was the smartest kid I knew, and I really looked forward to his visits. He didn't have the kind of smarts that adults admired, like smart in school or smart in knowing the books of the Bible. Brian just had ideas that would've never occurred to me.

One year, Brian had shown Kevin Perkins and me how to smoke. He took us to a field behind the high school that was a virtual grove of rabbit tobacco. Per Brian's instructions, with rolling paper cut from a grocery sack, we made six crude yet functional rabbit tobacco cigars. Per Brian's example, I threw up after we smoked them.

The next year (I think I was eight), Brian told me that rabbit tobacco was for kids. What we needed, he explained, were real cigars. Real cigars, he said, like he smoked in Birmingham.

"What kind of cigars did Granddaddy say he wanted?" I asked Brian innocently. We were perusing the tobacco rack in Rick's Rolling Store (think of it as a 7-Eleven on wheels). Brian had invented an elaborate scheme designed to fool Rick into selling us cigars. Since we were minors, I wasn't very confident in the plan, but it worked.

Brian answered, "Granddaddy said he wanted a pack of cherry-flavored Tiparillos and some apple-flavored White Owls."

We made our selection and handed them to Rick. "These are for Granddaddy," I said. "We aren't going to smoke them." Then I paid him with two nickels, one dime, and 122 pennies.

Years later, Rick asked if I remembered buying the cigars that day. He wondered if we'd gotten sick. "I just figured that turning green was prob'ly worse punishment than what your daddy'd a done if I'd a told him," he said.

Rick was right. We did get violently ill, and in that respect, I still do not see a great difference between real cigars and rabbit tobacco rolled in a paper sack.

The next summer, Brian had an idea that was actually enjoyed by many of the people in town. The animals, however, were not amused. We captured and released every pet we could safely grab but not before changing their appearances.

Brian put my sister's doll dresses on several of Mr. Michael Ted's cats. We caught Miss Luna Myer's white poodles and dyed them green. (Food coloring, by the way, does not wash out of dog hair.) Brian, with a black magic marker, connected the dots on the Peyton's Dalmatian while I gave their horse a gold tail with spray paint.

For a time, there were a lot of strange-looking animals walking the streets. No one really got upset either, except for Mrs. Perkins, and I can't say I blame her. Champ, her collie, was our masterpiece.

We borrowed my father's barber clippers and totally shaved the big dog. We did leave one strip of hair about two inches wide down the length of his back. Then we dyed it pink. Champ was a punk collie with a mohawk!

I got in quite a bit of trouble for that one. Mrs. Perkins called my dad and complained. I still think he was more aggravated about the dog hair in his clippers than he was about the actual dog, but the end result was the same—I got a whipping. Brian, meanwhile, was safely back in Birmingham.

The year I turned ten, Dad threatened to straighten me out with his belt before Brian arrived. He'd say, "That kid needs a little rawhide on the backside." Brian came anyway.

That summer we held our own carnival. We set it up in our backyard and charged a dime for any kid who wanted to come. The games all cost a nickel. We had ring tosses, bean bag throws, and a candy bar walk—which is just like a cake walk except that you use candy bars. We even had a BB gun range with one of my sister's teddy bears as the target and prize. I was nervous about that, but Brian bent the sights on the gun so that no one would win. No one did.

We made almost ten dollars at the carnival. Brian took about eight of that because, he explained, it was his idea. I didn't really mind though. It was a lot of fun right up until Steve Luker figured out that the BB gun was rigged and hit me in the stomach. My dad said I deserved it.

Considering the amount of trouble my cousin had gotten me into over the years, it's still hard to understand why I continued to listen to him. But I did. His powers of persuasion were of legendary proportions. Brian could take the most idiotic concept, and after fifteen minutes of his logic, I would think, *That sounds like a great idea!*

This particular gift of Brian's was why I now found myself running toward home in the middle of the night. "Do you think he saw us?" I said, wheezing.

"Who?" Brian asked.

"Mr. Hamilton," I snapped. "Who do you think I'm talking about? Do you think he saw us?"

"Nah. No way," Brian answered.

When we arrived home, we climbed through the window and into my bedroom. It was pitch dark inside the room, but we quickly got into bed. For a few minutes we just lay there. Then I spoke. "You reckon we'll get caught?"

"What's this 'we' stuff?" Brian said. "I didn't do anything. You threw the tomato, remember? And besides, I catch the bus tomorrow at noon."

I couldn't believe what I was hearing. Among my friends, it was all for one and one for all. No one ratted on anyone else; we didn't leave anyone behind, and above all, we went to the gallows together. But here was my own cousin—flesh and blood—bailing out on me! It was at that moment, after years of following him blindly, that I realized Brian was a snake.

The next day, I was glad to see him go. We took him to the bus stop at eleven thirty, and my mom and dad bought him some comic books for the trip. I wanted to punch him goodbye, but instead I shook his hand. "You're a jerk," I whispered through clenched teeth.

"I hope you get in lots of trouble," Brian replied and stepped onto the bus.

At lunch, it seemed as if Brian was about to get his wish. "Son," my mother said, "Mr. Hamilton called this morning. He asked if you would come over to the hotel sometime today." I almost choked. "He has a little work he wants you to help him with."

"Mr. Hamilton is a fine man," my father said. "I appreciate him coming up with jobs for you now and then. Work will keep a boy out of mischief." Then he said to my mother, "What's he needing done?"

Painting the porch or something," Mom answered.

"That's odd," my father said, "Tony painted that porch yesterday."

"Seems somebody messed it up last night," she said. "In any case, Andy, you go on over there to help after you finish your sandwich."

During the exchange, I scarcely breathed. Did they know? Had Brian told them? Maybe they knew because they were parents and they could read my mind. Why were they torturing me? Were they waiting for me to confess? Could they hear my heart beating through the silence? "Yes, ma'am," I said.

Mr. Hamilton was standing on the front porch with paint and

a brush when I arrived. It was as if someone had told him I was on my way. "Hey, Andy," he said, smiling. "Thanks for coming over." I grinned weakly.

"Take a look at this. Mrs. Hamilton and I painted this porch yesterday, and last night somebody threw a tomato on it before it was dry. Can you clean this up, sand it off, and paint it again?"

"Yes, sir," I answered.

"Great," he said. "Thanks for the help. Mrs. Hamilton was really hurt that someone would do this to us, so I'd like to go ahead and get it out of the way." With that, he turned to go inside.

"Mr. Hamilton," I said in a whisper.

He stopped, turned around, and peered over his glasses at me. "Yes?"

"Can I mow your lawn too?" I asked.

He put his hands on my shoulders, looked directly into my eyes and said, "Now why would you want to do that?"

I told him everything. I told him how we had sneaked out of the house, how I had stolen a tomato from the Carpers' garden, and how I had thrown it on his porch. I told him how sorry I was and how I hadn't meant to hurt Mrs. Hamilton's feelings. I may have even cried a little.

Mr. Hamilton shook my hand and said it was all forgiven. He said that he appreciated me being a man about it and owning up to what I had done. I repainted the porch, mowed, and got home in time for supper. My dad was waiting by the garage.

"You look tired," he said. "Clean up and go inside. Mom has soup on the table. Tomato, I think it is. By the way, Rick Carper called while you were out. He has some work he needs done tomorrow in his garden."

CHAPTER 5

For a moment, it looked as if he would be killed. Backed up against the red ice chest in the bow of the aluminum boat, he picked up a paddle to defend himself. Dick Rollins knew he deserved to die for what he'd done. And for that reason he almost put the paddle down.

Fearfully, he glanced behind him, searching for an escape. There was none—he was trapped. There was no help within a half-mile. Dick was all alone on the backwaters of Beauman's Pond. All alone in a fourteen-foot boat with his former best friend, Joe Bullard, who was now about to end his life.

Only seconds earlier, Joe had been a happy man. Casting a big purple worm on a hot afternoon with his brand new rod and reel, he set the hook on the fish of a lifetime. Both Dick and Joe watched open mouthed as the huge bass jumped clear of the water. "Ten pounds," Dick said breathlessly. "That bass'll weigh ten pounds."

"Get the net," Joe croaked. "She'll go eleven easy. Hurry up, Dick!"

As Dick extended the net, the trophy jumped again, right at the boat. Surprised, Dick made a swipe for the fish . . . and knocked it off the line. As the bass slowly swam away, Joe made a move as if he were about to dive in after it but turned toward Dick instead.

Dick actually felt nauseated. Had he done something minor, like burning down Joe's house or wrecking his car, all would have been forgiven. But this was not the case. What he had done was unpardonable.

Joe's eyes were wild as he stumbled over the center seat. "You did that on purpose!" he yelled. Moving toward Dick, Joe stepped on Dick's rod, breaking it in two. "And," he said, "I did that on purpose!"

By this time, Dick had backed up as far as he possibly could and was actually leaning out over the water. Wielding the paddle in front of him again, he said, "You're crazy, Joe. You know I didn't mean to lose that fish! Now get away from me or you're gonna turn this boat over!"

"How'd you know I was gonna turn that boat over?" Joe asked as they sat on an island in the middle of the swamp.

Dick glared at him. "Any idiot coulda seen it was fixin' to happen, you dumb-butt! Of all the stupid things anybody ever did . . . geez!"

Both men were soaked and miserable. When the boat tilted, water had come over the side and the craft literally sank from under them. Luckily, they had been near a small strip of land when the accident occurred, and that is where they ended up. Joe had saved only his tackle box. Dick still clutched the paddle.

"Are you still mad?" Joe asked.

"No," Dick answered.

"You still look mad."

"Well, I'm not."

"If you're not mad, then how come that vein on your neck is sticking out?"

"If you don't shut up, I'm gonna get mad!"

Both Dick and Joe blamed each other for the situation in which they found themselves. Dick's view was that Joe had lost control of himself and sunk the boat. Joe, on the other hand, was of the opinion that had Dick not lost his fish in the first place, he wouldn't have lost control.

"So, what do we do now?" Joe wondered aloud.

"I don't know," Dick answered. "It's too far to swim, that's for sure. And it'll be dark in an hour."

The swamp is located on the eastern side of Sawyerton Springs, on the far end of Beauman's Pond. Fed by the springs, it is more of a wooded lake than a swamp. The water there is deep and clear. Cypress trees and water oaks draped with Spanish moss give the place an isolated feeling; in fact, it is rather isolated. Stretching for several miles, the backwater is broken up only by a few small areas of high ground—most of which are less than fifteen to twenty yards long. It was one of those islands on which the two men were stranded.

Dick and Joe, best friends and neighbors, had fished together every Saturday for years. It was only the month before that they decided to go in partners and buy the boat that now sat at the bottom of the swamp. It had been outfitted with a ten-horsepower motor, two anchors, the works.

"I sure am glad you insisted on those extra large anchors," Joe said dryly.

"Yeah," Dick answered, "the whole rig did seem to sink a lot faster."

"What time you reckon they'll miss us?" Joe asked.

"Soon, I hope," Dick said. "I'm supposed to take Kathy to Foley tonight."

"Gettin' dark," Joe said. "Did you tell anybody where we'd be fishing?"

"Nope."

"Me neither."

Suddenly, Joe remembered the tackle box. He had put waterproof matches in one of the drawers years ago for just such an emergency. He quickly found them as Dick broke the paddle up to burn. A signal fire was just what they needed.

Unfortunately, wet paddles are unusually difficult to light, and this one was no exception. Joe held match after match on the soaked wood until each in turn burned his fingers and was dropped. Finally only one match was left.

"Here," Joe said, "You light this one. I've got some reel cleaning fluid in my tackle box. I'll pour it on the wood when you strike it. Maybe that'll help."

"Is it flammable?" Dick asked.

Unscrewing the cap, Joe replied, "I think so."

As it turned out, "flammable" was a rather weak description of the reaction of the fluid on the flaming match. Dick heard a loud "whomp," and suddenly everything was on fire.

The island was on fire. The air was on fire. Even the water was on fire. Fortunately, the pair had on extremely wet clothes. Neither Dick nor Joe could recall later whether they had jumped at the explosion or were actually blown into the air, but both agreed that the mushroom cloud was probably a first for Sawyerton Springs.

"You look strange without eyebrows," Joe said. Things had settled down again, and the paddle was now the only thing burning. "I wish I had some marshmallows. You hungry?"

"No."

"I am."

Joe tried to keep the conversation going. He was in a hole now, and he knew it. For a while there, what with the netting incident and all, Dick had been feeling pretty low. His smugness was returning, however, as the moron scales tilted toward Joe. Both were aware that a boat sinking and an explosion beat a lost bass any day of the week.

"Remember how many snakes we used to see on these islands?" Joe asked.

"No, actually I had forgotten that," Dick said, "but thank you very much for reminding me."

"Joe looked thoughtful, then said, "Guess this is probably what Gilligan felt like."

Dick glanced sideways. "What?" he said.

"Gilligan," Joe explained. "You know. Gilligan . . . on *Gilligan's Island*. They were castaways and we're kind of castaways, and I'll bet this is how he felt."

Dick stared at Joe.

Joe continued. "Did you ever wonder where they got all those clothes? I mean, it was just a three-hour tour . . ."

"I wish I had some clothes," Dick mumbled. "My pants are wet, my shirt is burned . . . that whole deal was really stupid, y'know?"

"I know," Joe said. "It was stupid. Like, why couldn't they get off that island? Here's the Professor—a guy who could build a radio out of coconuts and sticks—he couldn't build a boat?"

"I wish somebody'd build me a boat," Dick said.

"And another thing," Joe wondered, "What was Gilligan's last name?"

"Who cares?"

"No, seriously . . . Think about it. They never said! Was it Gilligan Smith? Or Gilligan Poindexter?"

Dick, in an effort to quiet Joe, said, "Look it was just Gilligan, okay? It was just plain Gilligan."

After a moment of silence, Joe said, "Yeah, I see. You're probably right. It was just plain Gilligan . . . like Oprah or Cher."

Dick rolled his eyes. "Will you shut up?" Then listening closely, he whispered, "I think I hear a boat." He stood up, but after several minutes said, "Well, no, I guess not. Sorry."

"That's all right. Mary Ann and Ginger always thought they were hearing boats too. By the way, I'm sorry I sunk ours."

"Well," Dick said with a rueful grin, "I'm sorry I lost your fish. She probably would have pushed twelve or thirteen pounds."

"No problem," Joe said, chuckling. "Maybe you'll hook her next time, and I can knock her off for you!"

Dick laughed. "By the way, how're we supposed to get off here? You haven't got a radio, do ya?"

"I ain't even got a coconut," Joe said, laughing. "Hey! Did Gilligan ever get off his island?"

"I don't know," Dick said. He wrinkled his brow. "Seems like the show just ended, and we never found out."

"That's what I thought," Joe said. "After all that time, they just come to the end of the story and don't tell you anything. Did they get off the island? Did they *not* get off the island?

"Geez, I hate to be left hanging!"

CHAPTER 6

GINNY WILLIAMS WAS MAD. IN FACT, SHE COULDN'T REMEM-
BER being quite so mad. It was just after eight o'clock in the morning, and she already had a headache. Sitting at the breakfast table in
her pink bathrobe, she held her coffee cup with both hands to avoid
spilling the hot liquid. Ginny was shaking. Ginny was mad.

Billy Pat, Ginny's husband, had pulled out of the driveway only
moments before. "Don't forget my white shirt," he said as he walked
out the door. "I'll need it tomorrow. And I can't meet you for lunch
today—got a meeting with Mike Wooley. Anything you need me
to do?" She shook her head. "Okay then," he said, oblivious to her
growing anger, "I love ya." He got in his car and drove away.

Ginny didn't answer until Billy Pat was around the corner.

"Yeah, right," she said and went inside. Pouring coffee into her
cup and all over the counter, she replayed in her mind exactly what
Billy Pat had said.

"Don't forget my white shirt." *How can I forget it,* Ginny thought,
*you leave it in the middle of the bedroom floor. If I forgot it, I'd trip and break my
neck. That's what I should have said. That would've been good. And why can't you*

meet me for lunch is what you ought to have told him. Thursday is supposed to be our day for lunch. Is meat loaf at the café once a week too much to ask? Yeah, well, you always have a meeting with Mike Wooley. I don't care if you have a meeting with the president of the United States, I'm your wife. That's supposed to count for something.

"Boy oh boy," Ginny said out loud, "if he were here, I'd tell him what he could do with that meeting. And the shirt!"

She pushed her chair back and stood up to begin cleaning away the breakfast dishes. As she balanced the cereal bowls for the move toward the sink, the top one fell, sending a shower of milk and glass all over the kitchen.

The word Ginny selected at that moment was not one with which she was totally unfamiliar. In fact, she had grounded her youngest daughter for saying the same thing just last week. But somehow when Ginny said the word, it was satisfying—rolling, as it did, crisp and clean from her lips. The word also perfectly described her mood.

Cleaning up the mess, Ginny tried to remember what else Billy Pat had said. What was it? Her eyes narrowed. She remembered. He had said, "Anything you need me to do?"

Yeah, there's something I need you to do, she thought. *There's quite a few things I need you to do. Starting with getting the garbage out on time. Mondays and Thursdays. The garbage goes out on Mondays and Thursdays just like it has around here for the last five hundred years. So that's one thing you can do. Remember the garbage.*

And how about not asking me twenty times "What's for supper?" I'll cook it—you eat it, okay? Mow the lawn more than once a month would be a good one. That way maybe the neighbors won't think we're growing hay.

As Ginny showered and dressed, she knew that what made her most angry was the fact that at that very moment, wherever Billy Pat was, he had no idea that she was even upset! In a way, it made her feel better to think of the things she would say if he were standing in front of her.

Lose some weight. How about that, fatso? Or, maybe you're going to start a Sawyerton Springs Sumo Wrestling League? Ginny smiled. That would have gotten him. Billy Pat had gained fifteen pounds since the end of May, and he was pretty sensitive about it.

You might stop snoring. That's something you could do. Also, don't mess with the thermostat after I've set it, quit belching at the table, and for once in your life, could you put the toilet seat down?

The phone rang. It was Elaine Green. Could she, she wanted to know, borrow Ginny's toaster? Elaine was having company and wanted to fix a nice breakfast the next morning. They didn't have a toaster, she explained, because Norman felt that the oven did an adequate job, and he didn't want to spend money on a luxury item like that.

Ginny wrapped the electrical cord around the toaster as she walked to her car. She had to deliver the appliance to Elaine, because Norman wouldn't spring for a second vehicle either. Fastening her seat belt, Ginny said aloud, "At least Billy Pat isn't cheap."

As Ginny drove to the Greens' house, she remembered the time she had mentioned to Billy Pat that their bed had been bothering her back. When they went to look at mattresses, he ended up buying her the bedroom suite she'd always wanted. "The best wife in the world deserves the finest furniture," he had said. She found out later that he used money he had been saving for a fishing boat.

Ginny visited with Elaine for a couple of hours then went to lunch alone. Thursday was her day for eating out, and she was determined not to miss it. She did, however, go to Norman's Groceteria in order to avoid Billy Pat at the café.

She sat at the corner table and ate macaroni and cheese with a salad. For dessert, she had lime Jell-O. Ginny had spoken to Norman when she arrived, but the place was relatively empty, so there was plenty of time to sit and think.

Why do I have to eat alone? she wondered. *It's not fair. He's always working—or says he is. Is one lunch a week too much to ask? He doesn't seem to care. Heck, he doesn't even know I'm mad.*

Ginny thought back to the night twenty-one years earlier when Billy Pat had proposed. He had been forty minutes late picking her up at her house, and she was furious. She didn't even speak to him until they were in the car. "I have been waiting forever," she had said.

"I'm sorry," he replied. "Work, y'know."

"Yeah, I know," she said, "all you think about is work. Ever since you got this new job, you live and breathe work. It's gotten to be the most important thing in your life."

Suddenly, she remembered, Billy Pat had swerved the car to the side of the road and stopped. Now he was mad. "Look here," he had told her, "it's not the most important thing in my life, but it'll allow me to do the most important thing in my life. This afternoon, when I asked your dad if I could marry you, I told him I would take care of you. I don't have a desire to work hard, I have a responsibility. That's different. I love you. This ring is for you."

Ginny had listened to him with her mouth open, tears rolling down her cheeks. "I love you too" was all she could say. "I love you too."

Sitting there in Norman's, Ginny wiped her eyes and blew her nose. *It's different now,* she reasoned. *We aren't kids anymore. Billy Pat owns his own business, a very successful one, and he doesn't need to spend the time with it that he does. It is different, isn't it?*

Ginny paid her check and left. She didn't talk to Norman on the way out. He had seemed kind of touchy earlier when she made a joke about the "luxury toaster" she had loaned to Elaine. He didn't even smile. *I'm glad Billy Pat can take a joke,* she thought.

When Ginny got home, she flipped on the television. "Soap operas," she grumbled. "I hate soap operas." Just the same, she sat down and watched.

For the next three hours, Ginny counted fourteen different people having affairs. As she turned the set off, she was glad that she didn't have that kind of thing to worry about. Billy Pat, she knew, was not that kind of man.

Ginny was about to start planning supper when Bonnie Pat, Janine, and Janelle burst through the door. The three teenagers kissed their mother and introduced her to a friend of theirs from school. Ginny recognized the girl as Robert and Cindy Wainright's daughter. Robert, her father, spent all his time hunting and fishing. Ginny had never seen him with his daughter.

I hope our girls know how lucky they are, Ginny thought. *Billy Pat's a great dad.*

Billy Pat had never seemed disappointed that he had no sons. He coached his daughter's softball teams, chaperoned their classes on field trips, and as they each turned fifteen, he insisted on being their first date.

Ginny puttered around the kitchen as she remembered Billy Pat giving the girls a corsage and taking them all the way past Foley to Elberta for dinner. He held the doors as they entered and even ordered for them at Wolf Bay Lodge, the nicest restaurant in town. He wanted the girls to expect the best from the boys they would be dating, and Billy Pat wanted to be the standard by which those boys were measured.

Lost in her thoughts, Ginny jumped when the doorbell rang. Opening the front door, she saw the florist truck drive away. There, on the porch, were a dozen red roses. *They must be for Bonnie Pat,* she thought. The Henley boy had been sending flowers a lot lately. Bending down to pick up the vase, she saw an envelope attached to the roses. The envelope had her name on it.

She brought the roses inside and sat down on the floor next to the couch. With the vase between her knees, Ginny opened the envelope and pulled out the card. In Billy Pat's handwriting, it read: "Lunch today was no fun. Mike is not nearly as pretty as you. I'm lucky to have a wife who is so understanding. I can't wait to see you tonight. I miss you. I love you. Billy Pat."

I was right, Ginny thought, as she put the flowers in their bedroom. *He didn't even know I was angry.*

And she was glad.

CHAPTER 7

As a boy, whenever the school year ended, August always seemed miles into the distance. Even on the calendar, June to August looked like forever. But in truth, the days of summer moved so rapidly when I was a boy that, even now, the memories blur. Only a few impressions of that time in my life are so distinct as to never fade—banana popsicles dripping over my fingers; the sound of metal skate wheels on the sidewalk; and the sheer, blood-curdling terror of "the rope."

My heart was pounding. For several minutes, I had not moved, and my friends were becoming impatient. "C'mon already—go!" Kevin Perkins yelled at me. He and Roger Luker were standing at the base of the oak in which I was precariously perched. With my left hand, I held a branch of the big tree while my right was wrapped in a death grip around a thick piece of bristly manila hemp.

The rope was a landmark in our area. It was tied to a sturdy limb almost ninety feet up in the old General's Oak, which stood on the banks of Beauman's Pond. Some of the older boys had climbed the tree several years before and, after securing the rope, also nailed a board onto one of the back branches. As they stood on the board, which was at least forty feet from the ground, they knotted and cut the rope to specifications.

Unfortunately, their specifications accommodated someone three or four years older and quite a few inches taller than the kids my age. An average-size teenager could comfortably stand on the board, grasp the rope with both hands, and leisurely swing out over the water before splashing down.

My first swing attempt had been only three weeks earlier when, because of my size, I hadn't quite been able to obtain the proper grip with both hands. Of course, this fact did not become clear to me until I was prematurely propelled into midair.

The weight and angle of the rope had pulled me (screaming) from the relative safety of the board platform. Desperately, I had scrambled to hold on as I bounced over each knot on the speeding rope, finally catching the last knot under my arm as I reached the edge of the water. Lacking the strength to hold on, my body sailed through a wild pyracantha bush and into the pond. My nose was bloody. I was bruised and scratched from head to toe—but I was alive!

Now, as I stood frozen, that memory came flooding back to haunt me. I let go of the rope and turned to climb from the tree. Suddenly, a single word from my friends below, spoken loudly and in unison, snapped me back to reality.

"Chicken!"

Well, there it was. I might have known it was coming. I would have said it myself had our positions been reversed.

"Chicken!"

For thousands of years, "chicken" has topped the list of the words most likely to provoke action from a boy. He might cry, he might bust you in the mouth, but if you call him a chicken, something will happen. That's certainly how I felt at that moment. Call me an ax murderer—call me a girl—but don't call me a chicken.

"Chicken!"

That did it. Furious, I turned around and made a wild dive for the rope . . .

Actually, the day had started off innocently enough. It was the Saturday before school was out for the summer. Kevin, Roger, and I met on our bicycles in the woods behind Henley's Hardware.

"Well," Kevin said, "whatcha want to do?"

"Just hang out I guess," I replied. "Or we could build a fort."

"Forts are for babies," Roger said, frowning. "I ain't buildin' no fort."

"What about G.I. Joe?" I asked. "G.I. Joe builds forts, and he's not a baby." *Ah, that got him,* I thought. *It was so nice to be right.*

Roger was a year older than Kevin and me, which to his way of thinking made him boss. We were somewhat skeptical of Roger and his ideas, because they always seemed to land us in trouble. The firecrackers in school? Roger's idea. The rubber band guns in church? Roger's idea. The water balloon in the library, the dog on the basketball court, the tape recorder in my dad's bathroom? Roger, Roger, Roger.

As I remember, it wasn't only the rope my father had warned me about. Roger had been included as well. "He's not as smart as you think," Dad lectured. "If he was so sharp, he wouldn't have gotten caught with the money from the Coke machine."

I had to agree with that. For several months, Miss Luna Myers had reported money missing from the Coke machine at the county health department. Everybody in Sawyerton Springs knew it was happening. The story had even been reported in the *Sentinel.* "Who," the editorial page demanded, "is robbing the only Coke machine in town?"

Why, Roger, of course. Or as the adults called him, "that Luker kid." He had been fishing change out of the machine with the blade from a hacksaw and a piece of duct tape. He would've gotten away with it too, if he hadn't wanted a pellet gun so badly. Roger walked right into Tom Henley's Hardware Store, picked out the one he wanted, and paid Tom forty-nine dollars . . . in quarters!

Roger was just that kind of kid. And that's what worried me as we sat there on our bikes. What would he come up with next?

"We could have a dirt-clod fight," he said, referring to an activity in which we collected lumps of earth from a freshly plowed field and threw them at each other.

"Nah," Kevin said. "I have on new pants. My mom'd kill me."

"Okay, then," Roger countered, "how about we go to the Methodist Church and catch some goldfish?"

Kevin and I looked at each other and shrugged. "Awight," Kevin said. "Sure—let's go."

The Beauman's Pond United Methodist Church kept a goldfish pool in its prayer garden, which occasionally proved to be a temptation not easily overcome by boys my age.

Since my father was the minister at the Baptist church, I knew I would be in trouble if we were caught, but seeing as how they were Methodist fish . . . well, it wasn't actually a sin.

As we pedaled off, however, I couldn't help thinking of what my father always said about Roger, "He's a good boy, but he needs some guidance." Then he'd say, "And if you hang around him too much, you're going to need some guidance too." That worried me. Guidance from my dad often came in the form of a size thirty-six, brown-and-black reversible belt.

I suppose I really should have stayed away from Roger. Kevin's parents too had warned him about "wrong associations." It was just that Roger had a special magnetism. Everything he came up with sounded exciting and wonderful. He could talk about snorkeling in a sewer, and by the time he was finished, you'd think it was a great idea.

We caught a couple of goldfish from the prayer garden pool, and having the good sense not to take them home ("Hi Dad, I stole these! How about a whipping?"), we walked down to Beauman's Pond and released them.

We stood there wondering if the goldfish would be devoured by a giant bass or catfish. "Or maybe," Kevin mused, "one day somebody will catch a ten-pound goldfish in this very spot. Goldfish filets, mmm boy!" We all laughed.

Suddenly, Roger looked across the pond and said, "Hey!

Nobody's on the rope. Let's check it out."

As Roger broke into a trot toward General's Oak and Kevin immediately followed him, I began a conversation with myself. *Is this something you should be doing?* I asked. *Might this possibly lead to trouble? Could you fake a sprained ankle and bail out now?*

Quickly, I made my decision. "Hey guys," I yelled, "wait up!"

When I reached the tree, Roger and Kevin were already under the rope, gazing up its incredible length. They were elbowing each other and chuckling. "Boy," Roger said to me, "you sure were scared when you swung from the rope."

"I wasn't scared," I said.

"Well, you sure were bawlin'," he said. He glanced toward Kevin, who was grinning weirdly.

"Who was bawlin'? I wasn't bawlin'," I said as I felt the heat rising on the back of my neck. I knew what he was doing, but I was powerless to stop it.

"Okay, if you weren't bawlin'," Roger continued, "and you weren't scared . . . do it again."

"What?" I asked, trying to keep the fear from my voice.

"Do it again," Roger demanded, "Ride the rope!"

Thinking quickly, I said, "I can't. I haven't got my bathing suit."

With a gleam in his eye, Roger went for his trump card. "You could take your clothes off—just go in your underwear. Nobody's around, but then . . . maybe you're a chicken."

What was I doing? I wondered as I pulled off my clothes. I knew better than this. *Just stop!* I told myself. *Just stand up for once and say, "Roger, I know what you're doing, and this time you won't get away with it."* But I didn't, and he did. Moments later, I climbed the tree. And that's the story on how I got up there a second time.

"Chicken!"

Diving wildly for the rope was not one of my short life's brighter moves. As I mentioned earlier, being identified as a member of the poultry family can severely affect the judgment of a young man. I was no exception. Leaping from the board platform was a mistake, and having retained some degree of intelligence, it was a mistake I recognized immediately. I missed the rope by more than a foot.

Tumbling to the ground, bouncing from limb to limb, probably didn't take more than a few seconds, but believe me, it was enough time to reconsider the merits of rope swinging. Oddly enough, my overriding emotion was not one of fear but of triumph. Oh, I was a goner! Of that I was sure. But at least my tombstone would read: HE WAS NOT A CHICKEN.

The point of this story is not that I might have been badly hurt (I wasn't) or whether or not my dad gave me a spanking (he did). The point, I suppose, is that as aggravating as certain kids are, they can still turn out all right.

Roger Luker is now a real estate salesman and the volunteer police officer in Sawyerton Springs. He's married with two children of his own. What most people saw in him as "trouble" was just creative energy.

Today, I am more likely to take an interest in a boy like Roger. That mischievous attitude and all those wild ideas are leadership qualities in a child. Steered in the right direction, that kind of kid will eventually make our world a better place . . . if he doesn't drive us all crazy in the meantime.

FALL

CHAPTER 8

THE FIRST COOL MORNING OF AUTUMN WAS ALWAYS punctuated by my mother's attempts to make me wear a sweater. "You need to stay warm," she would say. But I had been warm. I had been more than warm . . . I had been *hot* all summer long. I *wanted* to be cool. It was September! Now was the time for chill bumps on my arms and the smell of burning leaves. And corn dogs at the fair.

The 94th Annual Kemper County Fair closed its gates late Saturday night after a successful week. Tom Henley, for one, was glad it was over. "Good gosh-a-mighty," he exclaimed to Billy Pat Williams, "you'd have thought we had the only fair in the world the way people crowd in here!"

Billy Pat agreed. As this year's co-chair of the event, it was his duty to oversee the parking situation at the fairgrounds, which as he put it, was "a job and a half." For the first time ever, the steering committee had decided not to charge three dollars per vehicle, as had been done in the past, but to assess one dollar for every person in the vehicle.

This, everyone felt, was a much more responsible method of admission. It not only made sense financially, it would end the teenagers' attempts to pack ten to twelve kids in a single car.

By all accounts, the new parking rules were a success. Billy Pat thought so, because it all ran so smoothly; the committee thought so, because receipts were up 17 percent; and the teenagers thought so, because eight kids really can fit in the trunk of an Oldsmobile.

The fairgrounds are actually just a big field running parallel to Highway 59 on the outskirts of Sawyerton Springs. Parking is, of course, just off the highway with the main gate immediately beyond that. The livestock tents have traditionally circled the midway, allowing people to sense the "atmosphere" of what a county fair is supposed to be in the first place.

Intermingled with the livestock tents were the craft, home goods, and school science tents. An additional tent was used this year for local merchants to display and sell their wares.

On Tuesday, judging was held in the home goods competition. Jan Jones won first place for her tomatoes and green beans, Glenda Perkins took a first with her ginger snap cookies, and for the eleventh year in a row, Best in Show was given to the same person: Annie Rae Edwards. She won in the pickle division with a recipe calling for a hint of allspice. The recipe was given to her, she revealed, by her mother Clara, who lives in North Carolina.

The area schools did a wonderful job with the science tent and their theme: "The Future is Ahead of Us!" Two hundred eggs in one booth were being hatched by an electric blanket, and a corner of the tent was dedicated to showing us how we will shop in the future by using our televisions. The sign, made of Elmer's Glue and red glitter, proclaimed: INTERACTIVE TV—ARE YOU READY?

The big hit of the science tent, however, was reserved for Todd Rollins. Only a junior in high school, Todd made a water-powered lawn mower. Hooked to a garden hose, it would cut the grass and water it at the same time. Besides having his picture in the *Sentinel*, he won a fifty-dollar gift certificate from Norman's Groceteria.

The Future Farmers of America, in conjunction with the 4-H

Club, competed for trophies and ribbons on Wednesday. Cows, horses, sheep, pigs, goats, chickens, and even rabbits were available for viewing.

The auction on Thursday was lively, and more than a few animals were purchased by the parents of the children who raised them. This is a yearly phenomenon. It makes no difference how often Mom and Dad said, "You know, of course, what cows are for . . ." or "That's the part where we get bacon . . ." When the man from the meat-packaging plant is bidding on old Lulu, a sobbing child often prompts a parent to reach for the wallet.

While the tent for local merchants was enthusiastically accepted by the local merchants, most of the fairgoers gave it mixed reviews. Miss Edna Thigpen of the *Sentinel* wrote, "Why should we go to a fair to see Norman's groceries in a booth? If I want to see one of Billy Pat's foreign cars, I'll go to his car lot! Henley's Hardware with a display of hammers and screwdrivers? Who cares? And what was Mike Martin thinking?"

Actually, quite a few people wondered what Mike Martin was thinking. Mike of Mike's Mortuary, had a rather large selection of coffins and tombstones on display. Most people stared for a moment, blinked, and hurried on past. George Cossar, with his fried chicken stand right next to Mike, was furious: "He's killing everyone's business, no pun intended. This is a fair for gosh sake, what does he think people are going to do? Does he think people will say, 'Well, heck, honey. While we're here, let's go ahead and buy a casket.' Geez!"

With the exception of the local merchant's tent, very little has changed or is new since I was a boy. The Kemper County Fair started in the early 1900s as a time for farmers and their families to get together for a week and celebrate the harvest. Only years later were midway rides and attractions added.

When I was an eighth grader, the rides and attractions were the fair. And there was something about the people who ran the rides and attractions that provided an element of danger to life in a small town.

Fair week was the only week during the year when people in Sawyerton Springs locked their doors. The roustabouts and carneys were thrust at us as an example of what could happen to our lives if we didn't do our homework. "Look at that child," our parents would say. "How'd you like to have that many mosquito bites on *your* legs?"

Often, being hurried down the midway, someone was pointed out as a product of an ill-spent youth: "You could end up with a job like that if you don't watch it."

To my way of thinking, "a job like that" didn't seem half bad. I even practiced what I heard one man saying. I really had it down. The gravelly monotone sounded good. I'd sit with my legs crossed at the knees, hunch up my shoulders and say, "She's right behind this curtain, friends. She's waiting just for you. She's inside, and she's alive— Nina, the Headless Girl. A freak of nature, the good Lord's only mistake—Nina, the Headless Girl. Ladies and gentlemen, boys and girls, one thin dime will buy your time—Nina, the Headless Girl."

Over and over I'd do it—just like the man on the midway had. The last time I did that particular bit was the first time my father heard it. Actually, there was no one in the church at the time, and I still think the microphone made it sound great.

The fair of my eighth grade year was special. It was the first time I was to be allowed freedom on the midway—no adults. Kevin Perkins, Lee Peyton, and I would have run of the place. We each had five dollars we had saved for the express purpose of blowing at the fair.

Our plan was to budget a small amount for food and use the rest for the important stuff. No rides. Heck, our parents let us get on the rides. We wanted to taste the forbidden fruit—the sideshows and the games!

None of us had ever been permitted to enter a sideshow, and we could only wonder why. Lee said it was because of "nakedness." "Sure, Nina ain't got no head," he said slyly, "but I'll betcha she's got everything else!"

The games, on the other hand, were forbidden for an entirely different reason. They were impossible. "You can't win," my father told me again and again. "The people you see carrying stuffed animals around are "plants." Are any of your friends loaded down with prizes? No. Why? Because you can't win."

What does it take, I would think, *to knock over some milk bottles with a baseball? How could you not pop a balloon with a dart? I could do it. I would do it.*

On Friday night, after eating several corn dogs each, we headed through the horse tent to the midway. There, grooming her barrel racing quarter horse, was our English teacher from the year before. "Hi, Miss Wheeler," we said as we passed. "We're going to get you a teddy bear."

She smiled and said, "Thanks, guys. I appreciate it, but I already have a teddy bear, and besides, the way those games are set up, you can't win."

With that quickly in and out of our minds, we continued on to the midway. We checked things out for about thirty minutes then regrouped near the pig tent to discuss our options.

"Well, I'm definitely knockin' over the milk bottles," I said. "What'r you guys gonna win at?"

"Darts for me," Kevin said. "I guess I'll get my mom that stuffed snake."

"Aren't we going to see any sideshows?" Lee asked. "I'd kinda like to see, Larry the Lizard Boy."

So that was first on the agenda. Larry, the Lizard Boy, turned out not to be so much a boy as a full-grown man. And, we agreed, Mrs. Trotter in the third grade had a skin condition much worse than Larry's.

We also saw Benjamin Franklin's brain in a jar and Sam Spaniel, the man with a face like a dog. But the best was Sheba . . . Jungle Queen—raised by gorillas, captured by scientists.

Sheba growled, jumped around her cage, and ate with her hands. Later, we saw her eating at the Band Boosters Hamburger Stand with Larry, the Lizard Boy. She was still eating with her hands.

Though I had almost three dollars left, I had only budgeted one dollar for knocking over the milk bottles. One dollar was not enough. Even at a quarter per try, those milk bottles would not fall down. "C'mon kid, you can do it," the man kept telling me. "A little girl just did." It didn't make sense. I threw hard. I hit them well, but they wouldn't fall.

Meanwhile, Kevin was tossing darts at balloons. When he finally popped three, he pointed to the big stuffed snake that wrapped around the booth, but the lady running the game reached under the counter and gave him a plastic doll. "The snake's for five wins in a row," she said, smiling. "Ready to try again?"

Lee had stayed with me and had tried the milk bottles several times himself. "If we threw together I'll bet we could knock them off," he mumbled. The man heard him.

"I'll tell you guys what," he said, looking around carefully, "since I want you to get that teddy bear, for three dollars, you can both throw at the same time."

We had him. We knew we had him. "Deal," we said and ran to get Kevin. Three dollars was all we had between us, and as we laid it down, we laughed. Our parents would be so surprised when we did what they said could not be done.

As Lee and I took careful aim, Kevin counted. One, two, three, throw! We threw. Both balls hit squarely, but the bottles did not fall down. They rocked, they moved, they tilted, but they didn't fall. "Tough luck, guys," the man said. "Try again next year."

"At least," Kevin remarked as we walked away, "we don't have to hear our dads say 'we told you so.'"

Lee stopped. "Do you really think they'd rub it in if they found out?" he asked.

"Mine would," I answered.

That following Sunday morning, my father preached about the end of the world. "There will be explosions," he said, "and tornados and earthquakes. And nothing will be left standing." Then my dad looked at me and smiled. "Nothing," he continued, "but those three milk bottles at the fair."

CHAPTER 9

In small communities, the "everyone knows everyone" thing can work in your favor or against. On one hand, there is the availability of wisdom, watchfulness—even help, should it come to that. But on the other hand, there are no secrets. And if you didn't want to know what someone else *thought* about what you are doing or thinking or wearing . . . well, you "might oughta" be living somewhere else.

Here are a few examples. Two weeks ago, according to the *Sawyerton Springs Sentinel*—"The State's Eighth Oldest Newspaper"—the descendants of John Paul and Bernice Eleanor Kaiser got together recently for a family reunion. It was held in the fellowship hall of Beauman's Pond United Methodist Church. All the Kaisers under seventy years of age brought a covered dish. This was page-one news.

On page two, there was a mention of Katrina Anderson's recent bout with allergies and a detailed account of Granger Clark's heart attack under the headline: GRANGER IN BAD SHAPE! The article went on to give Dr. Peyton's assessment of the situation, which was "stable," but also included Miss Luna's opinion that "things don't look good for Granger."

Page three included a list of those people whose subscriptions to the *Sentinel* had expired—their names in bold print. Everyone knows that their name will stay in the paper until they renew, so they usually pay up quickly.

The lone exception is Roger Luker. He and his wife, Carol, have been on the list for almost nine years. He told Billy Pat Williams that he never read the *Sentinel* anyway and wasn't about to pay a "fine" to the paper's eighty-three-year-old owner, Miss Edna Thigpen, just to get his name removed like everyone else did. "So that is that," Billy Pat remembers him saying. And after nine years, most people in town believe he meant it.

The Classified section, also on page three, offered babysitting by Janelle Williams, Billy Pat's daughter, and a flashing arrow sign for rent by Tom Henley. Foncie Bullard is selling a full set of Mossy Oak camouflage (boots included) that her husband Joe gave her for Christmas, and someone is looking to buy a good bird dog. Whoever it is, however, did not include a name or number in the ad.

At the bottom of the page, as always, were the advertisements. And as always was the note from Miss Edna asking "the reader" to ignore the ad for a "home-based business."

"Warning!" her note says. "This scheme comes from somebody in Michigan and is probably some kind of swindle. They do, however, pay one hundred dollars for the space and have never been late with their money. As long as that continues, we will run this ad, but as responsible members of our community, we feel the need to inform you, our public, that they are more than likely crooks. Signed, The Editor."

In addition to the usual talk generated by the newspaper, most of the excitement this month has been centered on the *Sentinel*'s back page—page four—where the announcement about the band fundraiser was printed.

For the past three years, the Sawyerton Springs High School Marching Barracuda Band has been raising money for new uniforms. Now less than eight hundred dollars shy of their goal, most people believe this will be the last year the kids will have to appear in borrowed outfits. "Won't it be great," Ginny Williams said to the Band Mothers Committee, "to see all twenty-three of our kids in uniforms the right size and color?"

The Band Mothers Committee consists of Ginny, Betty Jo Cosser, Foncie Bullard, and Melanie Martin. Only Ginny actually has a teenager in the band, but Betty Jo and Foncie have younger children who will one day benefit from the program, and Melanie is Mike Martin's wife.

Mike, the owner of Mike's Mortuary, is also the band director. Several years ago when the principal, Paul Krupin, found out that Mike had attended college on a tuba scholarship, he asked him to form a band for the school. "C'mon, Mike," Paul pleaded. "At our home football games, a lot of people are leaving during halftime. We've got to have something to keep them there!" So Mike agreed to help.

When he began, there were no uniforms at all; therefore, during the first year Mike, had the kids wear blue jeans and white T-shirts with packages of cigarettes rolled up in their sleeves. They played fifties music so it would appear the clothes had been planned. During the third quarter of the last game of the season, however, Brad Rollins, the trumpet player, actually lit one of the cigarettes and smoked it. Soon after, Mike assured the band parents that he'd come up with something else.

And he did. The next year, the kids wore some old military uniforms Mike borrowed from the VFW and played patriotic songs. Then it was cowboy hats and country music. The game after that it was bathing suits and the hits of the Beach Boys. Since most of the band stayed sick for two weeks after, the decision was made to use the old uniforms of nearby Foley High until the money could be raised for their own.

The uniforms were not in the best of shape, and the kids hated wearing the colors of a rival school, but as Mike explained, "It's either blue and gold or the fever of a cold—take your pick." In any case, those are the uniforms still being worn by the Marching Barracudas.

"So, what do we do this year?" Ginny asked as she opened the meeting. "We sold chocolate bars and candles last year. Before that it was Christmas trees and brass-plated social security cards."

Melanie sipped her coffee and mused, "We've had car washes, spaghetti suppers, and Halloween carnivals. I like my social security card. Do you think that company could do church bulletins in brass? They would make great mementos."

"We could sell old clothes," Betty Jo suggested.

Foncie laughed. "Betty Jo, most of the people in this town are already wearing old clothes. I know I don't want any more!"

"How about a raffle?" Melanie asked.

"Nothing to raffle," Foncie answered.

"Well, we'd better come up with something," Melanie said, "or just divide the money up and give it back to everybody."

For a moment, the ladies were silent. Then Foncie's eyes widened. "*That* is a great idea!"

"What?" they all asked. "What is a great idea?"

"Remember that story in the Bible," Foncie said, "where the guy gave three other guys the talents?"

"Talents are like dollars, right?" Betty Jo asked.

"Right," Foncie said. "Anyway, he told them to take the talents and multiply them, and he rewarded the guy who increased profits the most."

"So what does that have to do with us?" Melanie asked.

"Don't you see? We can take the money we've already made, give everybody in town some money—say ten dollars—and see what they can do."

"It might work," Ginny said, looking at Betty Jo.

Foncie stood up. "It *will* work. Mel, withdraw all the money from the bank. Get it in tens. We'll stay here and make a list of people to involve. Hurry back!"

At first people were suspicious. It had been a long time since anyone had handed out ten-dollar bills on Main Street. But after an explanation from the band mothers, and particularly after the *Sentinel* came out, they all calmed down. Unfortunately, most of them also took a "wait-and-see" attitude.

The people who *did* choose to participate were told they had thirty days to do something with their money. "This is an investment in your town and in our children," read the copy in the paper. They were enthusiastic, but there was a very vocal group who disagreed with the concept altogether. They felt that this type of thing was the board of education's responsibility. And besides, they said, it'll never work.

"Who cares what they think," Mike told Melanie over lunch. "Anytime we try to do something great, the critics come out of the woodwork. They are really good at telling us what's wrong with something, but they don't ever actually *do* anything. It's like a guy who knows the way but can't drive the car. This idea will work if *we* do!"

It turned out that there were only seventeen people who actually participated in the project, and for a time, Foncie was depressed. But soon she saw the incredible results that can be achieved by a few people with a common goal.

Kathy Rollins took her money and bought flour and yeast. She made loaves of homemade bread and sold them all over town. When she sold all the bread, she took a little of the money, bought more flour and yeast, and repeated the process. At the end of the month, Kathy turned in $108. Glenda Perkins bought two white flowerpots, painted sunsets on them, and sold them for $15 each. She did the same thing seven more times and made $210.

Billy Pat took $10 worth of wood and made two walking canes. Ginny painted them, and by turning the money over several times during the month, they made $120. Janelle, their daughter, also took in an additional $55 doing needlepoint.

Tom Henley sold soft drinks in his hardware store. He made $165. Norman Green bought cat litter and cleaned oil from driveways at $10 a pop. He made $130. Joe Bullard, Foncie's husband, took a can of car wax and turned it into $420. Several of his friends said it was worth thirty-five bucks to watch Joe work on their cars. It was worth it to Joe too.

In fact, it was worth it to everyone. Sue Carper was so proud she was able to hand Foncie $89 that she had tears rolling down her face. "I know I don't have a child in the band," she said, "but thank you for letting me be a part of something this worthwhile."

As everyone turned in their money last Friday night, the seventeen people who stuck it out and made their ideas work were awed by what they had accomplished. As they laid the bills and change out on a small card table in the band room, they clapped and cheered.

Kevin Perkins: carved wooden dominoes, $100
Roger Luker: selling tomato plants, $105
Melanie Martin: prune cakes, $120
Mike Martin: homemade peanut brittle, $80
Paul Krupin: shining shoes, $180
Carol Luker: manicures, $140
Wade Ward: refinishing furniture, $345
Jerry Anderson: painting deck rails, $100
Rebecca Peyton: ceramics, $76

The Super Seventeen, as they had been calling themselves, raised $2,543, which was certainly enough to cover the band uniforms for their children. But as I see it, they did something far more important. Long after the new uniforms are tattered and faded, the children of Sawyerton Springs will remember the example of seventeen adults who found a way to make things work.

The critics turned their backs, the skeptics laughed, but the uniforms are bought and paid for. Never underestimate the power of a group of people who have a dream fueled by enthusiasm. Mike had it right when he told Miss Edna in an exclusive interview for the *Sentinel*, "Whether we think we can or we think we can't . . . either way we're right!"

CHAPTER 10

A FIST FIGHT ALMOST BROKE OUT IN SAWYERTON SPRINGS a few days ago. Tom Henley and Kevin Perkins, despite being neighbors and long-time friends, very nearly got into it. They were right on Main Street across from Tom's hardware store when it started.

"Well," Kevin said, "me'n Glenda are going to vote yes and just hope there are enough other intelligent people in town to push this thing through."

Clenching his teeth, Tom demanded, "Are you saying that I'm not intelligent?"

"Draw your own conclusions," Kevin retorted.

The next thing anyone knew, they were shoving like school kids and saying things like "Oh, yeah?" and "I dare ya." Thankfully, cooler heads prevailed, and the two were pulled apart before anyone got punched, but no one bothered to ask what in the heck was going on—everyone knew.

The whole thing started last Monday night when Roger Luker showed up at a town council meeting. Roger arrived late and sat near the back of the room.

Meetings of the town council have been little more than a social event for years. Time and again, people come to hash over the same old things—parking problems, littering fines, and property tax disputes. They all seem to enjoy it—just bicker a while, drink some coffee, and go home.

Roger waited anxiously for Rick Carper to quit arguing about the lack of a leash law in the city limits and smiled at Miss Luna Myers across the aisle. She and Miss Edna Thigpen were there to air their monthly gripe about the inconsistencies of garbage pickup. *Just about everybody in town is here tonight*, Roger thought to himself as he glanced around the room.

As he stood up to speak, his knees felt weak. Roger's wife, Carol, hadn't accompanied him to the meeting, because she didn't approve of what he was about to announce. Putting her out of his mind, he cleared his throat and said, "Members of the council, I'm Roger Luker of Roger Luker Real Estate . . ."

"Excuse me," Dick Rollins interrupted, "what company did you say you were with?" Everyone in the room laughed as Roger's face reddened. They all knew very well who he was and what he did in addition to being the only policeman in town. After all, Roger had grown up here. It just tickled them that someone they had known for thirty-seven years would feel compelled to announce his name and business every time he shook your hand!

As the room settled down, Roger ignored the snickers and continued. "I have," he said, "from an outside business interest, a proposal to build a golf course around Beauman's Pond and develop the Springs as a resort."

As if someone had flipped a switch, the room was instantly silent. Several men, frowning, rose slightly in their seats. Even the ladies working at the coffee table froze in mid-pour. You could literally hear everyone swallowing . . . hard.

If it was their attention Roger was after, he got it. He might as well have said, "I'm Roger Luker of Roger Luker Real Estate, and I'm here to steal your children!" The reaction would not have been any different.

From that point on, the meeting was an exercise in finger pointing and name calling until they all got tired and went home. Roger, having seen the handwriting on the wall, left within minutes of his announcement.

He gunned his squad car up the big hill on Cherokee Avenue and squealed the tires as he turned onto Keating. Passing Dick Rollins's house, he muttered under his breath, "Jerk," and reaching the last house on the right, skidded into his own driveway.

Roger slammed the screen door as he stalked inside, and to Carol, who was sitting on the couch with her arms folded, he said, "Buncha hicks!" Carol simply looked at him. Her lips were pursed and her gaze steady. She made no comment. "They're all a buncha hicks," he said a little louder this time. Carol still didn't say anything, so Roger went to bed.

Roger and Carol have lived in the same three-bedroom, two-bath house since they got married twelve years ago. They have two children—Ben, a three-year-old boy, and Kelsey, a baby girl. They have a good marriage, but their personalities couldn't be more different.

Carol is satisfied with her home, her town, her family, and life in general. Roger, on the other hand, is professionally bored. Since 1989, when he got his license, he has been the only real estate agent in town who never saw a house bigger than three bedrooms. For years, he has dreamed of the big deal, until out of the blue, Thursday a week ago, the deal walked through the door.

A distinguished-looking man wearing an expensive suit and alligator shoes showed up without an appointment and asked to see the springs for which the town was named. Did the springs flow from marsh or rock? Was the water pure? Who owned the springs? Who owned the land nearby? Explaining that he represented a large development firm in Atlanta, he described to Roger the type of area for which he was searching.

Roger immediately drove him to the springs. Located behind the Beauman's Pond United Methodist Church, the springs fed Beauman's Pond and provided water for the whole town. The springs, the pond, and 129 surrounding acres were deeded to the town by Thornton Beauman more than one hundred years ago. Technically, the town also owned the land on which the Methodist Church stood, but that had never been a problem.

After walking the property, taking some pictures, and talking into a little tape recorder every few steps, the man asked to be driven back to his car, which was still at Roger's office. As he made ready to leave, he turned to Roger and said, "We are prepared to offer a 5 percent ownership package and $700,000 to the town of Sawyerton Springs for the total parcel of land. The payment would be a one-time cash deal with the ownership package including residual revenues from a resort hotel and golf course. I'll need a commitment, in writing, two weeks from today."

And with that, the man drove away. Roger ran inside, locked the door, and quickly began calculating what his commission would be on $700,000. "Two weeks," he said to himself. "I have two weeks to get this done."

By nine on the morning after the council meeting, every man, woman, and child in town had an opinion about Roger Luker. To some, he was an economic savior; to others, he was just a greedy Benedict Arnold!

Billy Pat Williams and his wife, Ginny, were among those who liked the idea of development. "It'd be good for business in this area," Billy Pat said, "and besides, I always wanted to play golf."

Rick Carper was also for the deal. He carried golf balls in his Rolling Store and in seventeen years had not sold the first one.

Joe Bullard and Dick Rollins led the group of business owners who wanted to call the man from Atlanta, tell him no thank you, and then "just go beat the hell out of Roger."

Also committed to preserving the status quo were the ladies of the Genealogical Society led by Miss Luna Myers and Miss Edna Thigpen. They made signs and formed a picket line around Beauman's Pond. The signs were printed with slogans like "S.O.S . . . Save Our Springs" and "Golfers Gamble and Curse—Do We Want That Here?"

Miss Edna, as editor of the *Sawyerton Springs Sentinel*, dedicated an entire edition to the controversy. Included were pictures of families picnicking at the pond and comments by some of the townsfolk who were against the change. Dr. Lee Peyton said that if he'd wanted to live in a town with strangers, he would have moved to Birmingham in the first place.

Conspicuously absent in the paper was any opposing viewpoint. "I own the darn thing," Miss Edna said, "I'll put in it what I want!" And she did. The prize piece of writing, however, belonged to Miss Luna. In her weekly column "What's On My Mind," she really let everyone know. It was a scathing diatribe on developers, Roger Luker, and change in general. She even mentioned Satan several times. Near the end of her column, Miss Luna asked the question, "When the whole place is destroyed with swimming pools, tennis courts, and golf courses—what will be left for our children to do?"

Actually, Miss Luna did make an observation that most folks had overlooked. What about the church? The Beauman's Pond United Methodist Church had stood in the same location since the 1920s. Was it now in danger of being used as a clubhouse? "Or," Miss Luna wondered, "will the sinners just tear it down? And what about the cemetery behind the church? Will they allow us to dig up our loved ones, or will they use the headstones as hazards on the golf course like a sand trap or a lake?"

Yesterday, when the town council announced that the residents of Sawyerton Springs had voted unanimously to reject the offer of development, most people admitted that what was on Miss Luna's mind had sort of been on theirs too. Everyone had been waiting outside the meeting hall for the results, and even Billy Pat and Kevin expressed relief that they weren't the only ones to have changed their minds.

As the crowd was breaking up, Billy Pat yelled, "Hey, everybody, hang on a second!" As they all froze, Billy Pat turned to find Roger, who had been standing off to the side. Looking right at him, Billy Pat said, "The council just told us that the vote was unanimous." Billy Pat paused as his eyes narrowed. "Which means that you must've . . ." Suddenly, he grinned. "Well, at least tell us why you voted against yourself."

"I'm not sure," Roger said, smiling sheepishly. "I suppose it had something to do with my growing up here. I got to thinking about playing golf and tennis with my kids, and I realized that there are a million places to do those things. But, you know, there's only one place I can show them where I used to swing on a rope with my friends. There's only one place I caught salamanders with my dad. There's only one church I've ever been a member of. And," he said softly as he took Carol's hand, "there's only one place that I can show them where their parents got engaged. This is my hometown."

Well, of course, Roger is back in everyone's good graces. And he's no longer professionally bored. The town doesn't know it yet, but Roger has decided to build a course anyway. He has already made an offer on the land next to his real estate office, and the first tee will start within sight of his front door. It will be perfect for families—eighteen beautifully landscaped holes of miniature golf.

CHAPTER 11

"I'M NOT A KID, YOU KNOW. I AM NINE YEARS OLD."

Those were the last words I said to my mother before I ran away from home. I don't remember the specific crime she had committed that precipitated my leaving, but I am certain—even now—that she was being unreasonable.

I was mature. I had a girlfriend. I was learning to burp like my dad. I had even smoked a cigar once. Okay, it was made out of rabbit tobacco and a piece of grocery sack and it made me sick, but my point was this: I was in the fourth grade. I had been around.

But my mother treated me like a kid. I couldn't believe it! So I decided to run away.

It was an adult decision. I carefully considered it for five minutes. I had the time. It was Saturday, so school wasn't a problem.

The thing about running away is that if it's to be any fun at all, you have to have someone to run away with. Mike Rawls was visiting his grandmother, so he was out. Mike's little brother couldn't keep a secret anyway, so it was probably just as well. Sharon Holbert would've been good, but she was a girl, and I wasn't about to run away with a girl. I liked Sharon, though. She could run faster than I could, and for a girl, she was a pretty good guy.

The obvious choice that day was Kevin Perkins. There were three reasons. First, his parents worked on Saturday, so they weren't home. Second, he lived on Cherokee Avenue, which was on my side of the four-lane highway I wasn't allowed to cross. And third, he would do what I said. This, I figured, was a very important quality in a partner. After all, whomever I took would almost certainly have the opportunity to "spill his guts" to my parents if we got caught.

I still can't recall what my mom had done that made me mad that day, but as I left the house, I gave her "that look." Even now, as I write this, I don't know exactly what that look looks like. All nine-year-olds did it. They still do. That look is a combination of anger, disbelief, and fear that will appear on a kid's face as a reaction to something a parent has said. Parents don't like that look; therefore, when they see that look, they usually content themselves by saying, "Don't give me that look." That's what my mother said that day. "Don't give me that look." And I got on my bicycle, giving it to her for all I was worth.

Kevin came outside as I pedaled into the carport. I had playing cards in my bicycle spokes, so he had heard me coming. When I told him my plan, Kevin was all for it. He said he had been thinking about running away for several weeks anyhow.

The first thing we had to do was gather food for the trip. The absence of Mr. and Mrs. Perkins lured us to their kitchen. We were conscious of packing light; therefore, we took only staple items: dill pickles, potato chips, a pack and a half of Oreos, one loaf of white bread, a plastic bag of chopped and pressed ham squares that cost seventy-nine cents then and still does today, a bag of marshmallows, four boxes of matches for starting a campfire in case we had to sleep outside, a box of toothpicks for putting in our mouths while we sat around the campfire in case we had to sleep outside, and two cans of bug spray to use around the campfire in case we had to sleep outside.

As we left, Kevin also grabbed three wax harmonicas left over from Halloween eleven months earlier. As I recall, those bright

orange wax harmonicas were the only luxury items we allowed ourselves, and Kevin talked me into taking them. He explained that we
could chew one of them and play the other two around the campfire in case we had to sleep outside.

It was almost two-thirty in the afternoon when we left the Perkins's house. We would have been gone by two o'clock, but Kevin
had to find his dad's poker deck so he could put playing cards on
his spokes. We rolled out of the driveway and down the big hill on
Cherokee Avenue as the fifty-pound packs of food propelled our
speed to upwards of twenty miles per hour. With our banana-seat
bikes sounding like Harleys and the wind whistling through our
crew cuts, we yelled. It was a yell of freedom—a yell of sheer joy! So
this was what it felt like to be on your own. It was great!

About thirty seconds later, we ran smack-dab into one of life's
ugly metaphors. Just when the going was easy—just when everything was downhill—we had to go up the other side. I could feel the
romance leaving this adventure. There we were, two mature nine-
year-olds with one hundred-pound packs, pushing our bicycles up
the other side of Thrill Hill. The cards on the spokes weren't buzzing with the same intensity. Pop . . . pop . . . pop . . . . Was this
what it felt like to be on your own? It wasn't so great.

We stopped to rest at Bobby Dale's Lake. Gratefully, we slid the
two hundred-pound packs from our shoulders and collapsed under
an old pine tree. Not a lake in any sense, it would have been more
accurately named Bobby Dale's Area of Standing Water, but it har-
bored vicious hand-size bream and the occasional water snake. So
to a fourth-grader, it was a pond. It was also on the other side of the
four-lane highway that I wasn't allowed to cross; however, Kevin
had insisted on choosing our direction of travel. So much for my
being in charge.

About the time we finished our last potato chip, we realized
that we had nothing to drink. I immediately began daydreaming
about my parents finding me dead of thirst in this wilderness and
very much enjoyed that vision. Kevin shook me back to reality with
one of his bright ideas.

"We could chew pieces of wax harmonica," he said excitedly. "That would work up the saliva!" (I think Kevin used the word "spit.") "And anyway," he said, "that's what the Indians did." Right! I was beginning to think Kevin wasn't taking this whole thing very seriously. Even I knew Indians didn't have wax harmonicas!

Suddenly, we heard a car engine. As I looked up, my blood turned to ice water. It was . . . my mother.

"Uh oh," Kevin whispered, "she has that look!"

"That look," as it appeared on my mother's face, had a totally different meaning from the that look discussed earlier. And just like every child since time began, I knew exactly what that look meant: I was dead. I was a goner. Outta here. A ghost. History. Vapor. Mist. A memory.

She stepped from the car, and the first thing I noticed was the manner in which she approached us. She was . . . well, she was calm. Calm?! Oh God, save me! My mother was so mad that she was calm! Goodbye, Kevin! Goodbye, world!

"Put your bicycles in the trunk," was all she said as she picked up the three hundred-pound packs (one in each hand!) and started toward the car. She swung them effortlessly into the back seat, tied down the lid of the trunk, and escorted Kevin and me to the front seat, conspicuously neglecting her usual encouragement to "buckle up." All my mother added to the otherwise silent vehicle was the promise she always made when I was in trouble. "When I get you home, *you* are going to get a talking to."

As Kevin got out at his house, he never said a word to me. No "see ya later . . ." No "had a great time . . ." Nothing. I'm pretty sure he was too concerned about his own skin. He was afraid his mom was going to get "a call." A call is just one more thing kids have to worry about. It's the way one parent gives spy information to another parent. We were always caught in the middle. The way we usually heard the bad news was something like, "I got a call from Mrs. Jones today . . ." At least that's how the bad news would start.

The rest of the way to our house, my mother never spoke. She never even looked at me.

She allowed me several years that afternoon to contemplate my fate . . . and finally started the trial.

"I want you to know," my mother began, "that I am totally shocked by what you did today."

No surprise there, I thought.

"I can't believe," she continued, "that you would have such a blatant disregard for my feelings."

I wasn't certain what "blatant" meant. Wasn't that a cuss word?

"And to think that you took Kevin Perkins with you! Or maybe it was the other way around? Either way, you know better. I'll give Mrs. Perkins a call tonight."

So far, she hadn't thrown me any curves. It was all the usual stuff. Pretty soon, she'd be telling me what her parents would have done if she'd pulled some crazy stunt like this.

"Young man!" She was really getting wound up now. "Do you know what my parents would have done if I had crossed a four-lane highway?!"

Whoa! Hang on! Wait! Stop! Back up! I wasn't sure I had heard that last part correctly. Did she say something about a four-lane highway? I listened more carefully.

"You could have been hit by a car!"

Yesss! I couldn't believe it! What incredible luck! There I stood before her, a runaway, a fugitive from parental justice, captured and being tortured by "a talking to" and all she was going on about was crossing some dumb highway! Why, she didn't even know I'd been gone! I was blessed. That had to be it. It was a miracle from heaven!

Thinking fast, I ducked my head to hide a smile and tried to force a tear to my eye. Gladly, I would take the rap for highway crossing. Every kid in the world knew how low on the punishment scale that indiscretion ranked compared with running away. Now if Kevin would just keep quiet about what we were actually doing (and I knew that would be no problem; remember, he would do what I told him.) I was home free!

The rest of the afternoon and on into the evening, the world was a brighter place. My dad shot a few baskets with me when he got home, supper tasted good, and my sister actually verged on "human." Sometime around eight o'clock, my sister and I were playing Monopoly. Dad had even joined us. He usually played solitaire on Saturday nights, but he said some of his cards were missing. My mother's absence had barely been noticed when she entered the living room. She lingered in the doorway. My sister saw her first and quietly slipped away. I noticed my father looking at my mother. Then I noticed my mother looking at us. Wait a minute, she wasn't looking at us. She was looking at me! And she wasn't just looking at me. She was looking at me with that look!

"Young man," she said, "Mrs. Perkins just gave me a call."

CHAPTER 12

MICHAEL TED WILLIAMS PASSED AWAY LAST WEEK. ON October 22, he would have been ninety-five years old. He was tall and skinny and had been a part of the landscape in Sawyerton Springs for as long as anyone could remember. When I was a kid, we often stopped by Mr. Michael Ted's house after school. He was old then, but you'd never have known it. Always laughing, he lived alone in a big, two-story house off Cherokee Avenue—just him and his cats.

Mr. Michael Ted had more than ten thousand cats, or at least it seemed that way. There were cats inside the house, outside the house, around the house, and on the house. He had black cats, white cats, and every kind of cat in between. Funny thing, though, he actually claimed to hate cats.

"You give me a wet cat and a good kick," he'd say, "and I'll get forty yards out of one of them things! Sneaky jerks—communist is what they are. Always peeking around corners, spying on everybody. They're the rear ends of the animal world!"

"Well, why do you keep them?" we'd ask.

"I can't get 'em to leave," he'd fume. "I'll tell 'em to get lost every day, but they stay around to torture me. Don't ever try to tell a cat nothing, kid, because he ain't gonna listen."

For all the talking Michael Ted Williams did about hating the cats, he never adequately explained to anyone why he bought fifty-pound sacks of cat food. Or why he made toys for them. Or why he made them all sleep inside when it was cold.

There was one place in his house, however, where the cats were not allowed. It was an area the whole town knew about, because most of us had been through it. We younger people thought it was neat, but its very existence caused most of the adults in town to think Michael Ted Williams was rather a nut. I am referring to the Elvis Room.

Mr. Michael Ted liked Elvis Presley. No, strike that. Mr. Michael Ted *loved* Elvis Presley. He absolutely idolized the man.

It seemed strange to us that an older person would be so crazy about an entertainer like Elvis, but he was. "Bing Crosby and them guys never had a clue," he'd say. "Elvis did it all. He could sing, he could act, and he loved his mother."

The Elvis Room was at the end of the hall on the second floor. It was a shrine. Hundreds of pictures were stacked on shelves anchored by Elvis decanters or other figurines. Movie posters were on the walls—*Fun in Acapulco, Girls Girls Girls, Viva Las Vegas, G.I. Blues*, and *Clambake*—all framed nicely.

By the door, a filing cabinet held every single record the man ever made—every album and every 45—still in their original jackets. One hundred twenty-nine ticket stubs were neatly displayed on a table in the corner. Each stub was a reminder of particular concert attended by Mr. Michael Ted.

"That there's the scarf Elvis wore in Louisville," he would say as he showed someone through the room. "Real sweat on it too. See that stain? Here's a popcorn bag from Tallahassee. Somebody threw it on stage. Elvis kicked it off, and I caught it. I was right there—right in the first row."

Every now and then, one of the kids in town would say something mean about Elvis just to get a rise out of Mr. Michael Ted. It always worked. Once Dickie Rollins made a comment about prescription medicine and, I believe, actually used the term "druggie" before finding his left ear wrapped around the old man's index finger.

Elvis had migraines, Dickie was told, and suffered from several old karate injuries. And unless Dickie wanted to know first-hand how a karate injury felt, he was to keep his opinions about pharmaceuticals to himself!

When Elvis died in 1977, Mr. Michael Ted left his cats in the care of his nephew Billy Pat and headed to Memphis. We saw him drive out of town past the elementary school with tears rolling down his face. For three days, he stood outside the gates at Graceland, paying his respects with thousands of others.

He met a lady about his same age, Patsy Jones, from DeKalb, Mississippi. She had met Elvis once at a train station. Having missed her connection that night, she hadn't had any money to eat supper. Patsy showed Mr. Michael Ted the five-dollar bill Elvis had given her for food, and as he held the bill admiringly, he asked why she hadn't spent it. She had been too excited to eat, she told him, and besides, she added, it was the nicest thing anyone had ever done for her.

When he got back to town, there wasn't a trace of sadness in Michael Ted Williams. "Elvis was way too young to go," he explained, "but the young fellow had a good life. He helped a lot of people ease their loneliness, and I, for one, will always be grateful. We still got his music . . . so we still got him."

From that point until his own passing last week, Mr. Michael Ted actually increased his obsession with Elvis, but in a happy way. He would travel hundreds of miles to talk to someone who knew the singer, he bought and traded more memorabilia, and even held an Elvis dance every spring for the high school. Nothing but Elvis songs were played for the kids, who were all dressed like Elvis and Priscilla. Priscilla was, according to Mr. Michael Ted, the only woman Elvis ever really loved.

About a year ago, Mr. Michael Ted started giving away his cats. "I ain't real young anymore, y'know, and these fur balls need to be kicked around by somebody." Almost every person in town took a cat or two. We knew that he was preparing for the end. What we didn't know, however, was how prepared he actually was . . .

"I'll be stopping by the bank on the way in to work," Billy Pat said to his wife, Ginny, at breakfast Wednesday morning. "Everything is already set, I think, but the will said that the funeral instructions were in a safety deposit box." As the closest blood relation to the deceased, Billy Pat Williams had been named executor of the estate.

It was all very simple actually. The house and lot were to become the property of the Methodist Church. The contents of the house were to be divided between friends and family, except for the Elvis memorabilia. It was all to be carefully packed and shipped to DeKalb, Mississippi, in care of Patsy Jones.

Billy Pat arrived at the bank shortly after they opened and followed a teller into the vault. He unlocked box number 30024 and inside he found an envelope marked: INSTRUCTIONS. Slipping it into his jacket pocket, Billy Pat thanked the teller, left the bank, and drove directly to the only funeral home in Sawyerton Springs, Mike's Mortuary.

Mike Martin, the mortician, met Billy Pat in the foyer, took the unopened envelope, and assured him that all would be taken care of. "I'll call you after lunch with the final details," Mike said, "but let's go ahead and set the service for Friday at two o'clock."

Ten minutes later, as Billy Pat walked into his office at the Toyota dealership, his secretary held the phone out to him and said, "Mr. Martin is on the phone. It must be important, because he insisted on holding, and he has been holding for seven or eight minutes!"

Billy Pat wrinkled his eyebrows in a confused manner and took the phone. "Yeah, Mike, this is Billy Pat. What's going on?"

"Billy Pat? Did you read the instructions your uncle left for his funeral?" Mike asked.

"Well, no," Billy Pat said, "I never even opened the envelope."

Mike continued. "Did he, by chance, ever give you any idea of his plans?"

"No, I don't think so."

"Did Mr. Michael Ted's will say anything about the funeral?"

"Just that his instructions were to be followed," Billy Pat said. "What's this all about anyway?"

"It's about the biggest send-off this town has ever had. Or is likely to *ever* have. For God's sake, Billy Pat, get down here—you are not going to believe this!"

On Friday afternoon at two o'clock, Beauman's Pond United Methodist Church was filled to overflowing. In fact, I believe it safe to say that the entire town was there. Every man, woman, and child—even some people who weren't particularly close to Mr. Michael Ted. There existed an air of expectation one rarely experiences at a funeral. The word had gotten out.

Near the casket were rows and rows of flowers. Gorgeous sprays of carnations and roses surrounded sayings like "Gone, But Not Forgotten" or "In Our Hearts Forever." Near the steps of the church's pulpit was the arrangement from Miss Luna Myers and Miss Edna Thigpen. It was a plastic telephone encircled by purple gladiolas and white mums. Above the phone were the words: "Jesus Called—Michael Ted Answered."

Mike Martin stood to the side. He was horrified. He knew what was about to come, and it seemed to him almost indecent, but as was his custom, he had done exactly as the deceased requested.

Pastor Wade Ward sat in his chair on the pulpit. Crossing and uncrossing his legs constantly, he kept wiping his face with a handkerchief. Pastor Ward was nervous. Maybe it was the music. "Love Me Tender" was playing in the background. New things always made Pastor Ward nervous, and today, he was about to perform his first Elvis funeral.

Mike nodded at Terri Henley, who approached the pulpit to sing the first song. *This is nuts*, she thought. *A song like this at a funeral? Well, here goes . . .*

"You aren't anything but a hound dog, crying all the time. You aren't anything but a hound dog, crying all the time. You haven't ever caught a rabbit, and you aren't any friend of mine."

Terri sang the song. She wasn't happy about it, but she did it. It wasn't appropriate to use improper English in church, she felt, so she took the liberty of changing some words. "Well, they said you were high class, but that was not the truth . . ."

She also sang "Heartbreak Hotel" and "Teddy Bear." Several people snickered when she finished her last song and said, "Thank you. Thank you very much."

Then it was Pastor Ward's turn. "Brothers and sisters," he began, "we are gathered here to mourn the loss of a friend. He was a very unusual man . . ." Pastor Ward said later that that moment was the only occasion in his entire ministerial career that the whole congregation "amened" a single statement. As he finished his prepared words about how wonderful a person the dearly departed had been, Pastor Ward paused to say a silent prayer of his own. "Sweet Jesus," he muttered. "Get me through this next part."

Reading from a printed sheet of paper Mike had given to him earlier, Pastor Ward said, "And now, ladies and gentleman . . . the moment you've all been waiting for . . . from Sawyerton Springs, Alabama . . . Michael Ted Williams."

Mike Martin pushed the button on a tape player and started toward the coffin.

BAHHHHHHHHHHHHHHHHHHHM. BAHHHHHHHHHHHHHHM. BAHHHHHHHHHHHHHHHM. BAH DAHMMMMMMM! BAHM PAHM, BAHM PAHM, BAHM PAHM, BAHM PAHM, BAHHHHHHHHHHHHHHHM . . .

As the music from *2001: A Space Odyssey* filled the sanctuary, Mike slowly lifted the casket lid.

. . . BAH DAH DAH, DAH, DAH DAH DAH! DAH DAH DAH, DAH, DAH, DAH!

As the lid opened, the mourners (if indeed they could have been called that) stood up and moved forward to get a better look. At the loudest part of the song, Mike had the casket fully open, and as he stepped back, people broke into applause.

There, amid the flash bulbs popping was Mr. Michael Ted Williams. His hair had been dyed jet black. He was wearing fake sideburns and a gold tux. He looked good. In fact, that's exactly what everyone said. "Doesn't he look good?" He didn't look natural, but a few people said so anyway. Everyone did agree, however, that he looked exactly as he had intended. He looked like a ninety-four-year-old Elvis Presley!

It is an understatement to say that no one will ever forget Mr. Michael Ted. He was a great old guy who provided us with laughter even after passing. One can imagine him chuckling as he wrote down the instructions for his own funeral—the most amazing production any of us had ever seen.

There was one more time during the service in which the congregation applauded. It was out of respect and admiration for the old man. Applause is intended as acknowledgment of a job well done, whether that job is a show . . . or life itself. So it was fitting that the congregation stood as one, clapping and cheering, as the casket was carried out of the church.

And then, with a big smile on his face, Pastor Ward looked at the people and said, "Ladies and gentleman, you can all go home. Michael Ted has left the building!"

CHAPTER 13

"WHOOO STOLE MY GOLDEN ARM?"

At that moment, I was not happy with the decision I'd made that afternoon to spend the night in the old Hazey place.

"Whooooo stole my golden arm?"

Kevin Perkins held a flashlight to his face and was making an effort to scare me. It was working.

Suddenly, he shut off the light, grabbed at me, and screamed, "You stole my golden arm!"

In a split second, my hands were over my face. My leg kicked into the air as I lurched against the wall and screamed. Then, slowly, I gathered my composure and explained my actions, which had, obviously, been for the benefit of the story—the better to scare everyone else.

It was a lame excuse and Lee Peyton said so. The Luker boys—Steve and Roger—agreed as Kevin looked at me smugly. "You were spooked," he said. "You're always spooked when we come here."

He was right. I had been in the house a hundred times, but it still gave me the willies. Located at the end of a logging road behind town, the dilapidated old structure had been abandoned for years. It was covered with wandering fingers of kudzu and honeysuckle, which only added to its creepy appearance.

The house held a sinister attraction for kids. Despite the pitchfork murder that had supposedly taken place in the attic at one time, we simply could not stay away.

This night, however, was different. I could have easily stayed away. In fact, on this particular night, I would have rather been anywhere else in the world. Because this night was the 31st of October—Halloween.

For the first time any of us could remember, Halloween was happening on a Friday. That meant, of course, no school the next day. We were given permission by our parents to camp out in the Peytons' backyard. The tent was there. We, on the other hand, were not.

Somehow the five of us had goaded each other into spending the night at the old Hazey place. We considered ourselves too mature for dressing up and begging candy from the neighbors.

Not that we didn't get candy anyway. Every Halloween, it amazed us that there were adults so naive as to leave a bowl of candy on the porch with a note saying, "Take One, Please." Two or three spots like that and a kid was done for the night!

We sat in a tight circle, close together in what we had decided was once the living area. There was a crumbling fireplace at one end of the room with an ancient sofa nearby. Directly behind us was the small staircase that led to the attic. "Dad will have a conniption fit if he finds out about this," Roger said. We all looked at him.

Steve, his older brother, spoke first. "You know what I'm gonna do if he finds out?"

"Kill me?" Roger asked.

"Right," Steve confirmed.

We were quiet for a while. I, for one, was not enjoying myself and would have gladly paid Roger to go get his dad. The stories were beginning to have an effect on me. I had had enough golden arms, hooks left hanging on car doors, and ghost girls being picked up on the highway wearing prom dresses. I was ready to leave and was about to suggest it when Lee picked up the conversation. "Reckon why she did it?" he asked.

We all looked at him. We knew what he was talking about. In 1951, so the story went, Martha Hazey stuck her fourth husband, George, with a pitchfork in the attic.

"She must have been really upset," Lee said.

"Not as upset as George, I'll bet," Kevin said, laughing nervously.

"Her first three husbands died from eating poisoned mushrooms," I said, repeating what I'd heard from Charles Raymond Floyd at school.

"Well then, why'd she kill poor George?" Roger asked.

Steve smirked, "Prob'ly cause he wouldn't eat the mushrooms!"

"My dad said she cut off his head," Lee offered. In our hearts, we knew that Lee's father had said nothing of the kind—that Lee had fabricated this part of the story—but no one challenged him, because the information, according to Lee, had come from his dad. Crediting one's parent with a wild tale has always been the primary method for avoiding the scorn of peers. ("I didn't say it, my *dad* said it!")

"Martha Hazey," I mused. "What kind of name is Hazey?"

"I'll betcha God gave her that name," Kevin said, "because it rhymes with crazy. You know she escaped from an insane asylum."

Kevin made the statement as a fact. He was not asking us if Crazy Hazey had escaped—he was telling us that indeed she had. He continued. "She dug up George's head and still carries it around . . . everywhere she goes." I was about to tell Kevin that he was full of it when he added, "At least that's what my mother told me."

"Somebody saw her down at Henley's Hardware not too long ago," I said. "She was looking around in the pitchfork section."

The other guys looked at me. Their eyes were the size of silver dollars and their breath was coming in rapid bursts. They knew I was lying as well as I did, but as we embellished the tale, it was like an addiction—there was no stopping us. The tension became unbearable. Past the point of casually getting up and going home, we were terrified!

Suddenly, Roger began to sing, "Ninety-nine bottles of beer on the wall, ninety-nine bottles of beer. Take one down, pass it around . . ." As his quivering voice faded away, we felt even more uneasy. It had been a pitiful attempt to change the subject. Roger was embarrassed, and we were embarrassed for him.

Only Roger's brother, Steve, said anything to him. "Don't be so stupid. If you ever do anything that stupid again, I'll . . ." Without warning, Steve's face went white. His mouth kept moving, but there were no words—no sound. He was looking at a spot directly behind me.

I looked at Roger and Lee. Their eyes were now fixed on the same spot. Roger was on his back trying to push himself away with his legs. Lee didn't move.

Kevin started a weird moaning sound that seemed to be an odd combination of crying and begging for mercy. As Steve continued to mouth nonexistent words, I quickly turned around and almost fainted. There, sliding slowly through the window, was a pitchfork.

My mouth was like sand and my heart was about to come through my chest. It was true! All the stories we'd heard were true. There really was a Crazy Hazey. She really did kill her husband, and now she was after us! Why had I come here? Why hadn't I gone trick or treating with my sister? Oh, if only I was wearing my Lone Ranger costume, but it was too late—we were goners!

"Ahh!" Kevin screamed, "It's George's head!" Indeed, something that looked very much like a man's head had come flying through the window and rolled up against Lee's leg.

A large percentage of the time, when one speaks of hair standing on end, it is merely a figure of speech. In this case, it was not. Our hair did stand on end, we curdled blood with our screams, and before we left the house, we ran in place for a few seconds like mice in a cartoon!

We didn't stop running until we were safely in the Peytons' backyard. We were out of breath, we were still scared, but we were alive.

To this day, I have never experienced sheer terror to match that

Halloween. Even now, I break out in a sweat when I hear kids singing "Ninety-nine Bottles of Beer."

It wasn't until years later—I was in college—when I found out what had actually happened that night. My mom and dad had walked over to the Peytons' with my sister, who was dressed as a dog. As the adults talked in the side yard, they saw us leaving the tent. Dr. Peyton and my dad decided to follow.

They had waited outside the window of the old Hazey place, listening to us talk in the living room. When the time was right, Dr. Peyton stuck an old board slowly into the window. (This is where I differ with my father's version. I still swear it was a pitchfork. "Where would we get a pitchfork in the middle of the night?" my father said.) Then my dad threw a clump of roots into the room, and the rest is history.

Because of that night, I never went in the old Hazey place again. That, I am sure, is exactly what my dad had intended. If so, he accomplished his goal. Still, it was a mean trick for a grownup to play on a bunch of kids. It makes no difference that it was Halloween. It was dirty, rotten, heartless . . . and I can't wait for the chance to do something like that to my own boys one day!

CHAPTER 14

WHEN LIGHTNING STRUCK THE BIG OAK TREE BEHIND Norman's Groceteria, no one knew *what* had been struck, but there was no question that *something* had taken a direct hit.

As George Cossar jumped out of bed, his first thought was that Dick Rollins had finally blown up his gas station. George had warned Dick for twenty years about smoking near the pumps. Shaking the cobwebs from his head, however, he quickly realized that what he heard had been closer than Dick's station.

Melanie Martin screamed in her sleep when the lightning struck. The combination of the boom and her reaction to it propelled her husband, Mike, toward the ceiling. When he hit the floor, he was in his pants. They were on backwards, but they were on. Frozen in a karate stance, Mike was ready to fight. Exactly who, he was not yet awake enough to determine.

Roger Luker was parked in front of Henley's Hardware when the storm came up. As the lightning and thunder grew worse, he drove his patrol car toward home. Passing Norman's on the left, he saw the flash in his rearview mirror and thought the store had been hit, but as he wheeled around for a better look, he saw that the grocerteria was fine. The tree, on the other hand, was split down the middle.

Straining to see through the rain, Roger directed his headlights toward the old tree. From what he could tell, there was no fire to take care of—it was raining too hard for that, but come morning, there would be a lot of cleaning up to do.

Roger parked and waited under the overhang at Norman's for the rest of the guys he knew would soon arrive. In a town like Saw-yerton Springs, all the emergency services operate on a volunteer basis. There is a volunteer fire department, a volunteer ambulance crew, and of course, Roger is the volunteer policeman. As *loud as that was*, Roger thought, *everybody will be here.*

He was right. It didn't take long for George and Mike to show up. They were joined by Billy Pat Williams, Dr. Lee Peyton, Kevin Perkins and Norman, who opened the store and made coffee for everybody.

"I built a tree house in that tree when I was in the fourth grade," Lee said as he poured coffee for Kevin. "This is kinda sad."

"My granddaddy built a tree house in it too," George said.

Kevin tore open a packet of sugar. "That oak and the General's Oak over by Beauman's Pond are supposed to be the oldest trees in this part of the state. More than four hundred years old, they say."

"Who's they?" Norman asked.

"Oh, you know," Kevin replied, "they . . . everybody . . . seri-ously, this tree is over four hundred years old."

"Well, it's been here as long as the town has, that's for sure," Billy Pat said. "Ginny has a drawing my great uncle gave her of Main Street and College Avenue in 1852. The tree's on it plain as day. And it was big then."

"Four hundred years old," Mike said, shaking his head. "Well, we'll be cutting it up for firewood tomorrow. See you guys about eight?" They nodded, and after talking a while longer, drifted back home.

The next morning, the lack of darkness and rain made it easier to see what had happened, but it was no less tragic. The lightning bolt had taken the old tree right in the main crotch and literally split the trunk in two. One half remained upright as if nothing had touched it.

"Is there any way to save this part that's standing?" George asked Kevin as they walked around the tree.

Kevin shook his head no. "Too much trauma to the whole system," he answered.

Kevin was about to pull the cord on the chain saw when Roger yelled, "Hey, you guys! Come look at this!" He was pointing to a place in the main trunk about fifteen feet above his head. As they gathered around to look, Roger said, "It looks like glass."

Protruding about three inches from the white, shiny wood that had once been in the middle of the tree was the rounded edge of . . . something . . . and it did in fact appear to be glass. Upon closer inspection with a ladder, the object was determined to be just that. It was a greenish-colored jar, and there was something in it.

Examinations of the tree explained how the jar became entombed in the first place. Someone, years ago, had evidently placed the jar into a hollow in the tree and neglected to retrieve it. As the years passed, the tree simply grew around the jar and only the lightning of the night before revealed its secret.

The rest of the morning was spent carefully sawing and hacking the wood away from the jar. It was lunch time when Billy Pat finally separated wood and glass and held up the jar. The thirty or so people who had gathered to watch cheered. "Should we open it now?" he asked.

"Yes, do it!" they urged. Throughout the morning, among the gathering crowd, speculations as to what the jar contained had reached a fever pitch. The consensus of the group was "treasure." Exactly what kind of treasure was a source of disagreement.

Sue Carper thought it might be Native American gold, but Jerry Anderson, who is Choctaw, assured her that if his ancestors ever had gold in the first place, they wouldn't have stuck it in any tree.

Several people agreed with Pastor Ward's theory that it was

probably money from a bank robbery. However, no one was able to remember any bank that had been robbed.

Moonshine, gold, fishing worms, and a murder weapon were all discussed as possibilities, but when the lid was pried off the jar, there were only three pieces of paper inside.

The first piece was a picture of Mack and Edna Sawyer, the original couple to settle near the springs in 1838. The picture was dated 1864. Also in the picture were their daughters Joyce and Barbara and their son Thomas.

The second piece of paper was a plat of the town. As Bill Pat carefully unfolded it, he saw areas that were shaded and marked "Sawyer." The largest shaded area was the part of town in which most of the present businesses were located.

The final document to be extracted from the jar was a deed. The deed gave ownership of the shaded areas on the plat to any male directly descended from the union of Mack and Edna Sawyer. Any Sawyer land, according to the document, was to be surrendered upon demand. Furthermore, the deed provided for unauthorized sale of the property by demanding lease payments of a hundred dollars per year for interim use. It was signed by Mack Sawyer and notarized by Jefferson Davis, president of the Confederate States of America.

As they all pushed in to see the amazing contents of the jar, Roger said, "Good gosh-a-mighty! If that deed weren't so old, Kevin Perkins would own this town!" Everyone laughed. It was common knowledge that Kevin was the only living descendent of the founders.

"Yeah, that'd be a pretty good deal," Kevin said, chuckling. "I've always wanted to own a town."

Suddenly, Mike spoke up. He peered over his glasses and said, "Actually, Kev, I think you do."

While everyone had been joking about the deed and its implications, Mike had been reading the fine print. Mike looked at the crowd, noted their open mouths, and continued. "Knowing what I do about the law and having studied Confederate land holdings in college, there is little doubt what has happened here. Mr. Sawyer had this particular deed signed by his president toward the end of the Civil War. If you know anything at all about history, you know that deeds of this type were upheld by federal courts when the Union was preserved."

"So what does that mean to us, Mike?" George asked.

"Well," Mike said slowly, "it means that just about every business in this town owes Kevin around $130,000 for use of property, which, by the way, is still his."

They blinked then looked at Kevin, who said, "I don't take MasterCard, and I don't take American Express."

All that afternoon, the town was in an uproar. The deed was the only topic of discussion. Kevin had built almost every home in Sawyerton Springs—now he apparently owned them all as well. Everyone had an opinion about the situation.

Lee Peyton said that he was inclined to ignore it, but George pointed out that Lee's home was not among those in question. "Easy for you to ignore it," he said.

Roger offered to arrest Kevin on some trumped-up charge and "just put him the heck in jail." But no, they decided. There was Glenda and the children to think about.

Miss Luna Myers told everybody she ran into that the whole situation was "of the Lord. His hand," she said, "chopped that tree in half to reveal His will to us."

"I suppose you could see it that way," Pastor Ward remarked. "I just hope the Lord realized that he gave away *His* house, too!"

Meanwhile, Kevin had not indicated whether he intended to hold anyone to the terms of his newly found windfall. In fact, he had not been around town all afternoon. Being a contractor, he was busy inspecting Olive Harvey's lightning-damaged home outside of town.

Olive was a widow with four children, and now her home, which was barely adequate to begin with, had a hole in its roof. "I can pay you a little at a time, Mr. Perkins," Olive told Kevin as he surveyed the damage. "You know, I waitress at the café and I have several sewing jobs coming up."

"We'll get it done tomorrow, Olive, and don't you worry about where the money is coming from. I don't think this'll cost anything." Kevin left her standing there with tears running down her face. As he cranked up his truck, he hoped someone would be of a mind to help Glenda one day if something happened to him.

By the next evening, Olive's roof was fixed, and there was a new oven and freezer inside the house. The freezer was filled to the top with food. Olive's children were wearing new clothes, and each had a new winter coat. Olive had enough sewing jobs to last a year, as well as extra material for several dresses of her own.

Back in town, the people of Sawyerton Springs went to bed that night having bought their property back from Kevin for thirty-five dollars each. When he had explained the purpose of the transaction, many townsfolk argued that their land and homes were worth much more and insisted on making up the difference. There was even enough left to start a college fund for Olive's kids.

"What a great place to live," Kevin said to Glenda as he turned out the light. And as he swung the covers over both of them, he added, "Even if I don't own it anymore."

CHAPTER 15

EVERYONE AROUND THE DINNER TABLE SMILED AS PAT Ward put the last dish in front of them. "I know it's not much . . ."

The whole family laughed out loud. That statement had been made by Pat every Thanksgiving of their lives. Actually, there was enough food to feed an infantry division, but she always worried that there would be some poor soul who didn't get at least five helpings of everything.

This year, she had prepared the dressing a day earlier than usual to give herself more time with the grandchildren, but she only used that time to expand the menu. Besides the turkey and dressing, Pat had baked a ham, three pumpkin pies, and a sweet potato casserole. She made fried corn, cranberry salad, squash, rolls, butter beans, and three kinds of peas.

There was a time when family members would jokingly mention a favorite dish during the days before Thanksgiving. This was only a game—a challenge to see if their suggestion would end up on the table. It always did. They felt guilty about that last year when Pat cooked six different entrees and eleven desserts, so this year they kept quiet.

"Wade, please say grace," Pat directed as everyone bowed their heads.

"Certainly, Dear. Let us pray." And as they all closed their eyes, he began. "Dear Heavenly Father, we come to you on this day of Thanksgiving with gratefulness in our hearts . . ."

Wade paused. *This is ridiculous,* he thought. *How can I even say that? I don't feel grateful at all. I shouldn't even finish this prayer.* But he did.

Pat's husband, Wade, is more commonly known around Sawyerton Springs as Pastor Ward. He has led the flock at Beauman's Pond United Methodist Church for well over two decades now, but lately it has all seemed a bit much. It's not that he is old—he isn't. "I'm just tired," he told Pat this morning, "and frustrated. I've had it.

"It's not necessarily the church," he tried to explain, "or Rotary Club or my city council duties, or the grandkids. It's just . . . well, it's everything. I've had it." Pat understood. Lately, she had kind of had it too.

There at the dinner table, Wade sliced the ham and looked at Pat's Uncle Frank. Uncle Frank was seventy-four years old and a first-rate know-it-all. Uncle Frank also knew a million jokes, and as Wade finished the ham and started on the turkey, he told another one. *Another stupid joke,* Wade thought.

"So there's these cowboys," Uncle Frank was saying, "and as they rode into town whoopin' and shootin', there was this dog right in the middle of the street. One of them cowboys shot him right in the foot.

"A couple of days later, the cowboys was in a saloon. They was drinkin' and cussin' and playin' cards, when all of a sudden . . ." Uncle Frank's eyes got big. "All of a sudden, a shadow fell over the saloon. As the cowboys looked up, they saw the dog walking through the swinging doors. He had on a gun belt and a hat pulled down low over his eyes. A cowboy said, 'What do you want?' and the dog says, 'I've come to get the man that shot my paw!'"

Everyone screamed with laughter. "I've come to get the man that shot my paw," Uncle Frank said again, banging his hand on the table. "You get it, son?" he asked Wade. "You get it, don't you? I've come to get the man that shot my paw!"

Wade forced a smile. "I get it, Uncle Frank," he said. "Would you like some turkey?"

Wade had driven all the way to Foley to pick up Uncle Frank earlier that afternoon. He had missed the first quarter of the Dallas-Detroit game because Uncle Frank insisted on leaving the house at two o'clock sharp. No reason and no way to talk him out of it. Before he even said hello, Uncle Frank had asked, "Son? If Patty Duke married Gomer Pyle, what would her name be?"

Wade shrugged.

"Patty Duke Pyle! Get it? Duke Pyle? Patty Duke Pyle!"

On the way to the house, sandwiched between the jokes, Uncle Frank had asked Wade why he was driving a twelve-year-old car. "It was a piece of junk when you bought it," he said.

"It's what we can afford, Uncle Frank," Wade had answered, but inside he had been seething.

As the family ate and talked, Wade thought about the car. *Uncle Frank had been right. It was a piece of junk when he bought it. The salesman had told him as much when he sold it to him. "It will need repairs now and again" were the man's very words.*

I'm fifty-three years old, Wade thought. *I should not be driving a twelve-year-old car. Pat is forty-eight, and she's never had a car of her own.*

For the third year in a row, the church elders had voted down a $1,500 raise in their pastor's salary. Last Monday, Roger Luker had come to tell him in person. "We just felt that the money should go to foreign missions," Roger said. "After all, there are a lot of poor people overseas. And besides, it's not like you have to make a house payment—the church owns the parsonage."

Wade drifted back into the conversation on the giggles of another joke. ". . . so there was the fat lady, stuck in the window of the church. When the guy in the devil costume walked around to ask directions, she said, 'Mr. Devil, don't hurt me. I been going to this church for forty years, but you know I been on your side all along!'"

As everyone howled, Wade thought, *There's probably some truth in there somewhere.* Through dessert, Wade wondered if his church members cared more about poor people they didn't know than they did about his family.

That's right, Wade said to himself, *you do own the parsonage. Where are we supposed to live when I retire? Or am I just supposed to preach till I'm a hundred and keel over on the pulpit? Why can't I buy my wife new dresses? Or a diamond ring? Or a new car? And about the car we're driving now—one more year and the engine will die. Then the floor will fall out, and I'll be driving around town like Fred Flintstone!*

After dinner, the family helped clean up while Wade tried to herd Uncle Frank into the car. "If I can get him out of here," Wade said to Pat, "then I'll have something to be thankful for!"

Uncle Frank's jokes were becoming a blur, and Wade easily tuned them out as he drove. The kids were on his mind. They were always after him to do something. "Daddy, fix this. Daddy, can you and Mama keep the children? Daddy, we're a little short this month."

The city council thing was bugging him too. He hadn't even wanted the position, but everyone begged him to take it. They said, "You will be a moral voice for the community, Wade, please help us!" Now they were all mad because he had voted no to having liquor at their Christmas party. What did they expect?

After Wade walked Uncle Frank to the door and listened to four more jokes, he got back in his car and drove. Had he gone straight home, this story might have ended here (and in not too happy a fashion).

But Wade didn't go home. It wasn't until two the next morning that he rolled into his driveway. Pat had been frantic, but she knew her husband too well to push him for answers. She was relieved he was safe and glad to see that he was smiling. It was the first time she'd seen him really smile in days.

Wade apologized for worrying her. He said he hadn't meant to be so distant or to snap at her as he had done lately. He kissed her, looked at her, and kissed her again. Then he went to bed.

Pat might never have known what happened that night that caused such a change in Wade had she not found the letter. It was in a bottle, floating near the bank in Beauman's Pond. Pat was raking leaves behind the church when she saw it. Reaching the bottle with the rake, she unscrewed the cap, fished out the letter, and read:

Dear God,

It doesn't feel like Thanksgiving. At least I don't feel very thankful. In fact, I am fairly ticked off. If you asked me about what—I'd say "everything." I am so preoccupied with the things that are going wrong in my life that I am having a hard time seeing the bigger picture.

Lord, I'm going to sit here by this pond until you remind me of ten things I have to be thankful for. And please do it fast. Pat is going to kill me for being late.

1). I have Pat. She loves me even when I'm being a jerk to her relatives like I was today.

2). I have a home in which to live. Remind me occasionally of the people on the street.

3). My family has enough to eat. I know there are fathers who put their children to bed hungry.

4). I have people who care about me. There are many who don't.

5). I was born in America. With all our problems, this is still the greatest country in the world.

6). I can see and hear and walk and talk. These are things I rarely consider, but they are a priceless gift.

7). I have the opportunity to help people who are hurting. It is amazing how much good an encouraging word can do.

8). I have the seasons. They are a constant reminder of change. After the winter in my life, there is always springtime.

9). I have my children and grandchildren who depend on me. That is an honor, and I have learned to be dependable.

10). I have music, trees, a good bed, a pond to fish in, my health, a car that does in fact run, clothes to wear, time with my family, and in Uncle Frank, I have an unlimited source of jokes for my sermons. Thank you, Lord, even for him.

--Wade

WINTER

CHAPTER 16

THE CHARACTER OF MY HOMETOWN HASN'T CHANGED IN significant ways since I was a boy. Kids still stand up when an adult walks into the room, and most have gotten the message from several different directions that they are not—and won't ever be—the center of the universe.

Growing up takes time. And in a small town, everyone is involved in the process. A child can misbehave three streets away and be in trouble with their parents before they get home. Oh, and good luck trying to talk your mom or dad into believing that Mrs. Thigpen or Mr. Carper or any other grownup had misunderstood the situation. No parent ever got mad at a teacher for bringing a child's class conduct to question. It became obvious to most of us early in our lives that the adults in Sawyerton Springs stuck together.

And they still do. Even now, they may not all "loooove" each other, and it is true some don't ever occupy the same pew in church, but unembellished, quiet respect is always apparent. The people in Sawyerton Springs are as careful with each other's feelings as they are with each other's children. There remains a simple goodness here that has long evaporated in other parts of our world.

Thankfully, the flu epidemic that swept through the area the week after Thanksgiving is all but over. So too is the quiet gloating of those who, for whatever reason, were lucky enough to escape the experience. Back in October, vaccinations had been offered for a mere ten dollars by the county health department. Setting up shop in the fellowship hall of Beauman's Pond United Methodist Church, however, was not an overwhelming success.

People stayed away in droves. Most of the Baptists declined participation in what they considered just one more effort in congregational poaching by the Methodists. The Methodists rebuffed the opportunity because of the nurse.

Miss Luna Myers, now in her eighty-third year, has been giving flu shots for the county since God's dog was a puppy. She looked like she was 150 years old back when she was working for Doctor Peyton; and Lee, who got all his shots from Miss Luna as a boy and has now taken over his dad's practice, won't go near her. "She's so shaky," he says, "that there'll be five holes in your arm before she gets the medicine in. Every hole feels like it was made by a jackhammer."

Needless to say, the line for Miss Luna's services last fall was a short one. And that, in a nutshell, seemed to be why so many people were sick. Oddly enough, however, Sawyerton Springs was the only town in the tri-county area where anyone so much as felt bad.

At the Williams's house on Keating Drive, Billy Pat and Ginny are up and around again after several days of nausea, headaches, and what Billy Pat calls, "The Big D." And it's a good thing too, because Ginny had just about come to the end of her rope where her husband was concerned. "Ginny, get me a glass of water . . . Ginny, I need a blanket . . . Ginny, please let the dog out." *For God's sake*, she thought, *doesn't he realize that I'm sick too?*

"Shut up, Billy Pat. Get your own water!" That's what she wanted to say but didn't. Ginny felt it was her duty to be the strong one at times like these, so she poured his water and covered him with blankets—all the while feeling like the dog she was constantly letting in and out of the house.

Blankets and liquids aside, most people in town feel like they might not have made it through flu season at all had it not been for Rick's Rolling Store. The supermarket on wheels is really just an old school bus from Montgomery that was put out to pasture in 1986. Rick Carper, who drove it for almost fifteen years, said that if they were retiring his bus, then they could just, by gosh, retire him too.

So Rick bought the bus and painted it red, white, and blue. He took out the seats and bolted shelves and racks all over the inside. After stocking the bus with every imaginable item, Rick and his wife, Sue, set out for Sawyerton Springs. It was Rick's dream to somehow be of service to his fellow man. "And what better way to be of service," he had said, "than to bring food to a hungry town."

Today, of course, there's Norman Groceteria on College Avenue, but when Rick and Sue arrived almost two decades ago, they were the only game in town. They sold soap, salt, pencils, vegetables, macaroni noodles, bolts of material, knives, candy, and even Sue's homemade pepper sauce. When you heard that big bus engine whine to a stop with those loud air brakes, all you had to do was go outside with your laundry basket, fill it with whatever you wanted, and your shopping was done for the week.

When Rick's Rolling Store first hit the streets, no one knew quite what to make of it . . . or why it was there in the first place. There seemed to be an abundance of theories. "They came from Montgomery to spy on us" was the most popular choice, though no one could actually think of anything Montgomery might want to know.

As a point of historical significance, the reason Rick and Sue choose Sawyerton Springs as their new home was quite simple. First and foremost was the fact that everyone in town had to drive twenty minutes to the nearest grocery store. But the sign at the edge of town had sealed the deal.

In 1953, when the sign went up, the town council had a tremendous argument about what the town's slogan should be. Every town, after all, needed to have one. It gave a place identity and a feeling of pride in what they were. Several of the council members, acknowledging the fact that Doctor Peyton had just opened his office, were pushing for "Sawyerton Springs—Gateway to Medicine." They were voted down, as was the contingent that wanted "Sawyerton Springs—Speed Limit 25." What they settled on was "Sawyerton Springs—A Town You Will Like." That is the slogan that welcomed the Carpers years ago, and though it has been repainted several times since, the same sign is still standing today.

The grand opening of Rick's Rolling Store has never been forgotten. Rick somehow managed to run over two dogs and a cat the very first day. By the next week, another dog, another cat, and Jerry Anderson's right foot had all fallen victim to the store on wheels. "Thank God the man didn't open a Wal-Mart," someone remarked. "He'd have wiped out the town!"

Before too long, Jerry, the animals, and the rest of the population had all gotten used to our town's new addition. As people became acclimated to shopping on a bus, Rick and Sue were gradually accepted and welcomed as friends. Rick was always quick with a joke and generous with free candy for the kids while Sue enjoyed talking with the customers wherever they stopped. Sue's pepper sauce had been such a hit that she frequently offered a monthly special of her homemade jam, bread, or anything else she produced in her spare time.

Nowadays I suppose one could say that time has caught up with Rick's Rolling Store. What with Norman's Groceteria having a larger selection and an *actual* Wal-Mart out on the bypass, people aren't as inclined to buy from Rick and Sue. But they are a part of the town, and you don't forget your own, so everyone still patronizes the bus occasionally. It's mostly little things like tape or a hairbrush, but folks make the effort because they remember when the Carpers made an effort for them.

If Rick heard that Mary Ann Winck was looking for Barq's "Red" Cream Soda to put in a special ice cream recipe, he'd make a note, and the next week he'd have it.

Or if Sue found out that Austin Adams liked bread 'n' butter pickles, that would be her homemade special of the month. Once when Miss Luna Myers fell and broke a hip, they carried her, lying in the aisle of Rick's Rolling Store all the way to the Foley Regional Medical Center—twenty-seven miles! People don't forget a thing like that.

When everyone fell ill last month, Rick and Sue were a godsend. Back and forth, all over town, morning, noon, and night. Aspirin to the Rollins, four bottles of Pepto-Bismol for Billy Pat and Ginny, and juices for the Cossar children. The chicken soup that Sue had made from scratch also continued to be a big seller just as it had been when it first came out—a couple of days before the town got sick.

As I mentioned earlier, most families buy their staples at Norman's and as an unspoken gesture of appreciation continue to buy and consume whatever Sue's special happens to be that particular month. Near the end of January, Rick's Rolling Store was stocked with Sue's chicken soup. She had made it with celery and carrots, a few mushrooms, and of course, chicken. On the jars, she had written in black Magic Marker, "salt and pepper to taste."

Within a week, well over half the soup was sold. It was obviously a good time of the year for that sort of thing, and despite the fact that it had an odd flavor, most people ate what they had purchased and enjoyed it. It was about that time when Lee Peyton began seeing his first cases of the flu. And it got bad quickly. Whole families were coming into his office together. "There's really nothing I can do," he told them. "Just go back to bed, and it will run its course. One more thing," he added, "eat some chicken soup—I hear Rick's Rolling Store has it this month."

And so they did. Sawyerton Springs bought every single jar of chicken soup on that bus. Rick managed to put away a jar for Sue and himself in case they came down with the bug, but other than that, they were sold out. "You know, honey," Rick said as Sue made the list for restocking, "this is the best month we've had since Norman opened up his place. I hate to take advantage of a bad situation, but your chicken soup is doing the trick for everybody."

It certainly looked that way. Within three or four days of a family's last jar, they were up and around. "Yessir," Dick Rollins told Billy Pat over lunch last week, "it's a good thing we bought a case of that soup. We kept eating it and eating it until we ran out. Wasn't long after—we were okay."

"Same thing at our house," Billy Pat responded.

Dick continued. "We'd never even have thought about using the soup to help us get well if we hadn't eaten it the night we all got sick."

"Same thing at our house," Billy Pat nodded.

"My girls didn't want to eat it, though. They said it tasted weird. I told 'em, 'so what if it did . . . eat it all.' I said, 'there's starving people in India that'd love to have it'." Dick paused, thinking. "Heck," he said, "that soup did taste weird."

"Same thing at our house," Billy Pat said slowly and the two locked eyes. Suddenly, a wave of realization washed over them like the nausea had done a few days before. No one had the flu. The soup was bad! They had gotten food poisoning.

As they checked around town, it was pretty much the same story with everyone. The Henleys, the Wooleys, the Wards, even Lee Peyton's family had all become deathly ill eating Sue's chicken soup. The people who didn't eat the soup never got sick. The people who did eat the soup got sick, ate more soup, and stayed sick until the soup was gone.

I talked on the phone last night to several of the people who were affected, and a curious thing has happened. They've decided not to say anything about it. "It's not as if they did it on purpose," Kevin told me.

"No real harm was done," Foncie said. "They were only trying to help."

Ginny Williams was concerned about Sue. "It would kill her if she thought she'd hurt us."

So that's Sawyerton Springs. It's no wonder the town doesn't have a lawyer—they don't need one. No one has stopped buying the homemade specials from Rick's Rolling Store. The Carpers need the business. People have, however, stopped eating what they buy.

But it's not viewed as a waste of money or dishonest in any way. It's just that Rick and Sue are important . . . and so are their feelings.

But the story doesn't end here. In fact, I believe there to be a sequel occurring as I write. Billy Pat and Dick ran into Rick downtown just this morning. "How's it going, Ricker?" Billy Pat asked. "Where's Sue?"

"Aw, she's visiting her sister in Birmingham," Rick replied, "so I'm being a bachelor."

"Want to come for dinner?" Dick asked. "Kathy and the kids would love to have you."

"No, but thanks anyway," Rick said. "I'm just planning to stay home and watch a little TV. It doesn't look like I'll catch that flu bug everybody else got, so I'm going to eat the last of our chicken soup. I never got any of it. Did you guys enjoy it?"

"Oh, yeah," Dick said, "we ate it all."

And with a smile on his face, Billy Pat added, "Same thing at our house."

CHAPTER 17

"EVERYTHING OKAY AT SCHOOL TODAY?"

I was ten years old and in the fourth grade at Sawyerton Springs Elementary. Every day for four years, my father had asked the same question after school.

"Yessir," I answered as I threw my books on the kitchen table and headed for the refrigerator.

"How's Mrs. McLoyd?" he asked. He always asked that.

"Okay, I guess," I said. I spotted Christmas cookies and brought them to the table.

"Is her hip still giving her problems?" he asked.

"Unh-unh-unh."

I answered in "kidspeak," a language known only to children and used specifically to denote a lack of interest in whatever an adult is talking about. Spoken in a hurried manner with varying tones "unh-unh-unh" means "I don't know."

"How can you not know?" my father asked. "Don't you see her walking around? Does she limp?" I shrugged. "Honestly, son," he continued, "I don't know how you find your way home. You don't pay attention to anything!"

He had a point there. I did occasionally walk past our house on my way home from school. It wasn't that I didn't pay attention—it was that my mind was on other things. I had an imagination that worked overtime.

I was not on the same wavelength as my father. Our thought processes did not coincide. He once looked at me after I had done something and asked, "If everybody jumped in the fire, would you jump in the fire too?"

I answered him with an "unh-unh-unh," but I distinctly remember thinking that if everybody jumped in the fire, then, yes, I probably would jump in too. I didn't say that, of course, because I knew that it was not the reply he was looking for.

Fathers say things that sound ridiculous to their children. Fathers are simply not aware that they are dealing with a totally different frame of reference. For instance, my dad used to say, "If you don't straighten up this minute, I'm going to wear you out, and I don't mean maybe." I could never figure out who "maybe" was. Did my dad spank him sometimes too?

Another thing he'd say after most of his speeches was, "Do you hear me?" It was inconceivable to me that he could believe I might not be able to hear him. He was usually six inches from my face—I could not only hear him, I could smell him too.

Dad got up from the table. "Hurry and do your homework," he said. "We leave for church in exactly one hour."

As the minister's child, I was at the church every time the doors opened. This was a Wednesday, which meant dinner at five o'clock in the fellowship hall, SonBeams for children under twelve at six, and prayer meeting at seven. And my parents had choir practice for an hour after that.

Usually during choir practice, I went home with the Perkinses to stay until my parents were through, but on this particular Wednesday night, things changed.

"Mrs. Perkins has a sinus infection," Mom said as we drove to church. "And I can't miss rehearsal tonight with the Christmas

Cantata coming up. So after prayer meeting just walk on home."

"By myself?" I asked.

Dad glanced my way. "Yes, you'll be fine," he said. "You're old enough to stay by yourself for a while. Just lock the doors when you go in, and don't let anyone inside for any reason. We'll be home right after choir." He smiled and patted my leg.

I was thrilled. "I'm going home by myself tonight," I announced at SonBeams. "I'll be all alone—and that means with no one else around."

Sharon Holbert stared at me with her mouth open. She was impressed, I could tell. "Yep," I went on, "it'll be just me, all alone, watchin' TV, eating peanut butter . . . being a bachelor."

"Won't you be scared?" Steve Krotzer asked.

"Nah," I said. "My mom and dad figure I'm kind of grown now. Being scared is for kids."

Later that night as I walked home, I smiled as I remembered the look of admiration on my friends' faces. It wasn't until I was in my own backyard that I noticed it was darker than usual. The house stood there, just as it always had, at 1505 Randal Road. But now, somehow, it seemed different.

For one thing, it seemed bigger. *Huge* was the word. Stepping onto the porch, a bird fluttered out of the camellia bush beside me. For a second there, it looked like a bat. "Aieee!" I yelled before I identified the sound. *I'd better get inside*, I thought. *There could be bats out here. No sense taking chances.* Bats, I knew, would make nests in your hair, lay eggs, and you'd go crazy. I'd seen that on TV.

I'd put the house key in my shoe before I'd left church, because I didn't want to lose it. Grown-ups did not lose keys, and I had too much other stuff in my pockets to risk a mix-up.

In my right pocket, I had two and one-half marbles, a rock, a spring from a ball-point pen, and three rolls of caps. In my left, I had an eraser, an air valve from an inner tube, two peppermints that had been out of their wrappers for a week, and a penny that had been smashed with a hammer.

I pulled the key out of my shoe and unlocked the door. As it opened, the door creaked. It was a long, low, creepy creak I had never noticed before. Slipping inside, I slammed the door shut so it wouldn't creak, and it rattled the house. Something fell in a bedroom and crashed to the floor. I locked the door behind me and listened . . . to silence. *Did something fall because I slammed the door?* I wondered. *Or did something else (or someone else) cause it to fall?*

Slowly, I tiptoed down the hallway—dark rooms to the left and right. My heart was beating so hard, I was afraid I would have a heart attack, whatever that was. I could see hands reaching out for me from the rooms. Probably the hands of John Dillinger and his gang, whom I had seen that very afternoon on TV.

There was a light on in my room at the end of the hall. When I got there safely, I saw that my autographed picture of Lassie had fallen to the floor. As I stopped to pick it up, I froze. I had almost put my hand within reach of the dark place underneath my bed.

I was certain that someone was under there. I knew, of course, that there was a sleeping bag, an electric football game, and my mother's sewing stuff under the bed already. *But,* I thought, *there might also be room for a man. A big man named John Dillinger, who had recently killed a bunch of orphans.* I felt sure that if I ventured too close to the bed, his big, orphan-killing hands could drag me under. Maybe he would even cram me into the sleeping bag and sew it shut with my mother's stuff.

Quickly, I got my BB gun from my closet. It looked real enough, I concluded. Sneaking to the side of my bed, I suddenly jammed the BB gun underneath and said, "Okay! I know you're under there, and I have you covered! Come on out."

Fortunately for me, John Dillinger did not crawl out from under the bed. I put the gun away and started down the hallway.

I stuck my hands in my pockets and tucked my elbows in. I wanted to present as small a target as possible for anyone who might grab me from one of the dark rooms. Reaching the living room, I sat back down on the couch, hands still in my pockets, and admitted to myself the obvious. I was scared.

I was nervously fumbling around in my pockets when . . .

pow-pow-pow-pow! I dove to the floor. What was happening? Pow-pow-pow! John Dillinger! With a Tommy gun just like on TV! Pow-pow-pow! When the noise stopped, I was crouched on the floor with my eyes wide open, but the only smoke in the room was coming from my pocket, because the three rolls of caps had exploded.

I stood up straight; the silence I had endured was now replaced by a ringing in my ears. Moments later, my parents entered the house. I was so glad to see my mom, but I was relieved to see my dad. My fear melted away. "Everything okay?" they asked. "Had I been scared? Why wasn't I ready for bed?" My home was noisy again—just the way I liked it. I was safe.

Now, looking back, I realize how often I did not understand my father. We were two very different people. But it was comforting to know that he was always there when I needed him. It was a great feeling growing up with a dad who could make John Dillinger disappear just by walking into the room.

CHAPTER 18

"JUST HEAR THOSE SLEIGH BELLS RING-A-LING, TING, TING-a-ling tooo! Come on it's lovely weather for a sleigh ride together with yooou!" Terri Henley sang excitedly as she washed the breakfast dishes. At two o'clock that very afternoon, she was to lead the Sawyerton Springs Combined Church Choir Carolers in the annual Christmas parade.

Terri, an alto in the Grace Fellowship Baptist Church choir, has sung with the carolers for the past thirteen years. They are a mixture of voices from the Baptist church and Beauman's Pond United Methodist—a combination that produces an occasional disagreement about song selection. The Methodists, being more traditional, prefer carols like "O, Little Town of Bethlehem" and "Joy to the World" while the Baptists seem to be more of a "Frosty the Snowman" bunch.

Finishing in the kitchen, Terri mentally went over the song list. "Sleigh Ride" was first, followed by "Away in a Manger," "O, Holy Night," and "I Saw Mommy Kissing Santa Claus." Those four songs, she was certain, would cover the parade route, which was only three blocks long. *Even then,* Terri thought, *we'll have to sing fast.*

Across town at that very moment, Billy Pat Williams was explaining to Dave Winck the procedure he wanted followed for the Ping-Pong ball drop. Dave is a pilot from Foley who has his own airplane and a crop dusting business. Crop dusting being what it is in December, Dave has had to resort to other sources of income.

"Now look, Dave," Billy Pat said. "We have five hundred of these Ping-Pong balls, and they're all numbered. Some of the numbers correspond to a cash amount and some can be redeemed for items at specific stores in town. Of the five hundred, about fifty are actually worth something."

"Just dump all five hundred directly over the parade route," Billy Pat said, "but wait until about two thirty—the parade will be over by then."

The Ping-Pong ball drop was a new idea that the city council felt would add a little life to an event that had become rather tired. The council solicited donations from businesses in the form of cash or merchandise to be given away to any person catching a correctly numbered ball.

All over town, the merchants were offering items for the Ping-Pong ball drop. Tom Henley, Terri's husband, donated a rake and fifty pounds of horse feed from his hardware store; George Cossar sponsored ten balls with his two-piece (dark meat) specials from George's Fried Chicken; and Rick Carper donated a fifteen-dollar shopping spree aboard his Rolling Store. The big prize was fifty dollars from Mike's Mortuary, where cash had really been the only choice. Or as Mike put it, "A gift certificate probably wouldn't be appreciated."

By one thirty, most of the parade participants were milling around the side street by the Vine & Olive Hotel. Roger Luker, the policeman, was trying to line everyone up by yelling through a bullhorn. No one listened.

The carolers were first, followed by the Genealogical Society float. Next came Rick's Rolling Store carrying the Royal Ambassadors and the Girls Auxiliary from Grace Fellowship. The Daughters of the American Revolution (DAR) walked behind them, led for the twenty-seventh year by Miss Luna Myers.

The problem spot in the lineup appeared to be the next entry. Betty Jo Cossar had taken six dogs and hitched them to a small, homemade sleigh. Eliza, the youngest Cossar, was to ride in the sleigh and the dogs, of course, were not happy. Complicating matters were the papier-mâché reindeer antlers Betty Jo had tied to their heads.

No sooner than the dogs were hitched up, Kristy and Tony Hamilton pulled into line with their horse and buggy. Governor, the horse, took a bite out of the wreath attached to the Cossar sleigh, which terrified Eliza. She ran screaming from her position in line and was immediately followed by the dogs, who were chased by the members of the Sawyerton Springs High School Marching Barracuda Band.

After what seemed like forever, calm was restored and the parade got started. Tony Hamilton glanced at his watch. It was two thirty on the nose. "What idiot positioned us behind these dang dogs?" he hissed to Kristy as he smiled and waved at Pastor Ward on the sidewalk. "I don't know if I'm going to be able to hold Governor out of that sleigh much longer."

Suddenly, a shadow passed over, and they all looked up. Struggling to hold Governor, who was frightened by the noise, Tony hollered to his wife, "What's he doing here so early?"

"I don't know," Kristy yelled back. "But if he drops those balls now, we'll have a situation on our hands!"

"Don't worry about it," he said. "Dave's not that stupid. There's no way he'll drop five hundred Ping-Pong balls right into the middle of a parade."

But he did.

At first, Dave had been confused. *Hadn't Billy Pat said two-thirty?* he wondered. It looked to him as if the parade was still happening. *Oh well*, he decided, *Billy Pat specifically said two-thirty.*

Dave is known around town as a person who will do exactly as he is asked. *Exactly.* If you want him to dust the bean fields behind your house, you'd better tell him *exactly* which bean fields. Otherwise, Dave might dust the bean fields behind your house into the next county!

Dave was not a rocket scientist, but he was not in a rocket. He had five hundred Ping-Pong balls that he had been instructed to drop at two thirty. It *was* two thirty. Bombs away!

Dave lined up on Main Street, dropped the plane down, and hit the trigger. The noise of the plane was too much for the animals. The Ping-Pong balls floating unexpectedly out of the air and the knowledge that one was worth fifty dollars was too much for the people. It was bedlam.

The dogs panicked and ran into the crowd by the library. They tripped and tangled, falling over their antlers. Governor reared up and took the Hamiltons careening through Norman's parking lot, where Miss Edna Thigpen, who is deathly afraid of horses, hit him with her purse and sent him running back into the street.

The band, meanwhile, ditched their instruments and competed gamely with the Daughters of the American Revolution for the Ping-Pong balls. Dave, having dumped most of the balls between Henley's Hardware and Rollin's Gas Station, continued to dive on the spot watching the action.

Folks, normally easygoing and polite, were quite literally stampeding each other for the little white prizes. It was the suddenness of it all—the unexpected early arrival of the possibility of something free that did them in. Pastor Ward, on his hands and knees chasing a ball, was heard to say, "I can't believe I'm doing this." But he did it anyway. He captured fourteen Ping-Pong balls and won a root beer from Norman's.

All in all, most of the townspeople had pretty much the same luck. When everything was said and done, it didn't seem worth the effort. Tom Henley won his own rake, and between George, Betty Jo, and their three kids, they got back four of their dark meat specials.

As for Dave, he is blissfully unaware that the town will not be using his services next year. The city council is already looking for a new, safer tradition to start. One that doesn't require planes or objects falling from the sky . . . or Dave for that matter, who was not only paid for his efforts, but turned in the one ball that blew back into the cockpit with him—and made an extra fifty bucks.

CHAPTER 19

THE TEMPERATURE WAS HOVERING AROUND TWENTY-SEVEN degrees, which is cold for the Springs area, but not cold enough to keep Kevin Perkins indoors. For most of his life, he has hunted mallards, pintails, and woodies on the backwaters of Beauman's Pond, and as far as he was concerned, this was the most important time of the year—the last gasp of duck season.

Kevin was on his way to The Last Resort, a cabin deep in the woods that his father had built when Kevin was a boy. As he nudged his Jeep across a pine tree that had fallen in the dirt road, Kevin smiled. He would soon be meeting the whole gang. Every year, they spent this week together in the woods. And seeing as how this was December, their wives always had a collective fit.

Glenda had really given it to him before they left. It was the same things she said every year. "I can't believe you're leaving. Here it is the busiest month of the year. Do you realize how much has to be done before Christmas? Do you not have any consideration for me at all?"

Kevin frowned. He did hate to leave Glenda—at this time of

the year especially—but he simply had no choice. He was only doing what his father had done year after year. It was a tradition, and he was not about to break it.

Rounding the last curve in the muddy road, Kevin saw smoke coming from the chimney, then the cabin itself. It was only three rooms, and what with the green paint flaking, it looked abandoned. But to Kevin, Joe Bullard, Roger Luker, Billy Pat Williams, and Dick Rollins, it was a paradise.

The guys piled out the front (and only) door as Kevin parked. "How boutcha, old man," Joe said as he grabbed Kevin's duffel from the back seat. Kevin was "old man" to his friends. Not because of his age—he wasn't that old. It was what they had been calling him since the tenth grade when he began losing his hair.

Dick and Roger ran around to the other side of the Jeep, "We'll get your gun," Roger said.

"You guys leave my gun alone," Kevin shouted as he reached in and pulled the 12-gauge through his door. Several years before on opening day, Dick and Roger had removed the firing pins from Kevin's shotguns. The guns would not shoot, so Kevin was the designated caller for his buddies all day long. Kevin was a good sport about it, but he had not forgotten.

"Where's Billy Pat?" Kevin asked.

"Oh, he's a weenie," Roger said, laughing. "Ginny told him he wasn't going anywhere. She said that the garage had needed cleaning since August and that she'd be danged if he was comin' with us."

"I blew the horn at him when I drove by," Dick said. "He had a lamp under his arm." They all chuckled.

"He'll wish he'd have stood up to her in the morning," Joe said. "We're gonna get a thousand ducks!"

"You better be careful," Kevin said as he smiled and looked toward the woods. "You wouldn't want Jerry to hear you say that."

They all nodded. They certainly didn't want Jerry to hear anything about a thousand ducks, a hundred ducks, or even one measly duck over the limit. Jerry was the game warden.

Jerry Anderson and his wife, Katrina, live on Randal Road right behind Dick and his family. They go to Grace Fellowship Baptist Church where Jerry teaches Sunday school and Katrina sings in the choir. Jerry is active in civic affairs, and he is one of Joe Bullard's best buddies—eleven months out of the year.

During hunting season, however, Jerry has a reputation as a tough customer. "You wouldn't even know he's my friend at all," Joe told the guys. "The man takes his job seriously. He'd give me a ticket in a heartbeat."

"I am a conversation officer," Jerry would say. "I am paid to protect the laws of our state as they apply to game and fish. And I will do it. If my own *mother* shot a duck out of season, I'd write her a ticket." The whole town agreed that, yes, he would.

Jerry is a full-blooded Choctaw Indian, and he knows that gives him an advantage in the woods. Not that he is quieter or has a better sense of direction than the next guy—it's just that he is the only Native American most people in Sawyerton Springs have ever met, so everyone imagines that his skills are on a different level.

And he doesn't do anything to discourage their thinking. Occasionally when he is in the woods with a friend, Jerry will feel the ground and say something like, "Deer. Two. Came through about an hour ago. The big one has a nice rack." Then he'll just stand up and continue to walk as if he could tell you what they ate for breakfast.

Because of Jerry's devotion to his career, people are a little nervous around him during hunting season. It's not that they're intending to break the law. It's just that he watches so closely.

Inside the cabin, over supper that night, Jerry was still the topic of conversation. "I knew a guy one time," Kevin said, "who swore Jerry came up out of the ground to get him. Swore he just appeared."

"It's the Indian in him," Dick said. "Tonto was like that."

Roger looked puzzled. "Who?" he asked.

"Tonto," Dick answered. "You know, Tonto, the Lone Ranger's friend."

Joe spoke up: "You know the Lone Ranger killed Tonto."

"I didn't know that," Kevin said. "Why'd he do it?"

Joe smirked. "He finally found out what *Kemosabe* meant!"

Just then, Billy Pat walked through the door. "Well, well," Kevin said. "We didn't think we would see you this week."

"You had nothing to worry about," Billy Pat said as he sat down at the table. "I told Ginny that I was coming and that was that. 'Ginny,' I said, 'I'm running the show around here and if I want to go hunting with the guys, then I'm going hunting with the guys, and there's nothing you or anybody else can do about it. Goodbye, baby,' I said, and here I am."

Kevin, Joe, Dick, and Roger looked at Billy Pat for a long moment. Kevin spoke. "You finished the garage, right?"

Billy Pat nodded. "And the basement," he sighed.

The week went by fast, and the hunting was terrific. They never saw Jerry, but they were fairly certain that he was around. One reason they had gotten nervous about Jerry's presence over the years was the law about legal shooting light.

Legal shooting time actually began well after daybreak; a law most hunters in the area had decided was unfair. The ducks had already landed by the time anyone could legally shoot. Therefore, a man who wouldn't dream of shooting over the limit would often, without guilt, begin shooting as soon as he could see.

This was accepted behavior for the inhabitants of The Last Resort. They felt that an unfair law didn't really apply in their situation. Jerry, on the other hand, felt that it did.

"I'm going to get those jokers," Jerry told Katrina as they went to bed that night. "I hear them shooting early every day, but by the time I can locate and sneak up on them, it's legal to shoot. I've got to actually catch them in the act."

At two o'clock in the morning, Jerry sat up in bed. "I've got it. I'll beat 'em to the punch. See you later, honey," he said as he crawled out of bed.

Jerry planned to hide outside the cabin, waiting for the guys to wake up. Then, as they left to hunt, he would simply follow them to their duck blind and ticket them when they started shooting.

Slipping into position about fifty feet from the cabin door, Jerry shivered. It was almost three o'clock and pitch-black dark. He had a while to wait before they woke up.

As he sat there, hunkered down in some blackberry briars, it began to rain. It was just a drizzle, but soon Jerry was soaked and miserable. His only consolation was the glory of his mission. He tried to imagine what it would be like when he revealed himself to the lawbreakers.

Smile, I'll say, Jerry thought, *you're on* Candid Camera. *No, that's too much of a cliché. And the show has been off the air for thirty years. I could sneak up right behind them and blow on a duck call as loud as I can. But no,* he decided, *they'd probably turn around and shoot me.*

After exploring options for about an hour, Jerry determined that the best method of surprising the hunters would be to crawl up beside the blind and just stand to his feet. Jerry chuckled to himself. Whenever he did that, people looked at him as if he had come out of the ground.

At exactly 3:50 A.M., lights came on in the cabin, and Jerry was alert. He could hear Kevin singing "Rudolph the Red Nosed Reindeer" at the top of his lungs. Pots and pans began to rattle as Joe started the bacon and grits. Dick stood on the front porch and smoked a cigarette.

Turning to go inside, Dick flicked his cigarette butt in Jerry's direction. *I ought to stand up now,* Jerry thought. *I could get him for littering.*

At that very moment, Kevin came to the door. He leaned outside and yelled, "Hey, Jerry! Man, don't sit out there in the rain. Come on in and have some breakfast!"

Jerry's mouth dropped open. "Unbelievable," he mumbled as he stiffly rose out of the briars. Walking toward the cabin, he was almost in shock. Kevin shoved a chair toward him as he went inside. Joe handed him a plate.

Dick and Billy Pat sat on the other side of the table from Jerry. Neither could stop grinning. Roger slapped Jerry on the back and laughed out loud.

"How?" Jerry asked. "How could you have possibly known I was out there?"

"Should we tell him?" Kevin directed his question to the other men in the room. They nodded.

"Jerry," Kevin said, smiling, "we actually had no idea you were waiting for us. But in a way, I guess you could say we've been waiting for you. We've been calling you to breakfast for the past thirteen years!"

CHAPTER 20

IT IS ELEVEN DAYS BEFORE CHRISTMAS AS I WRITE THIS, and for the first time in several years, snow is forecast for Sawyerton Springs. The children, as one might expect, are thrilled about the possibility of an early Christmas vacation, but to the adults . . . snow is just a cold, messy version of a mild hurricane.

Miss Luna Myers has been organizing the emergency relief effort for the Grace Fellowship Baptist Church. She compiled a list of all the men who have four-wheel drive trucks and has asked that CB channel 72 remain open for stranded townsfolk.

Rick and Sue Carper have stocked the Rolling Store with all kinds of non-perishables—in addition to the batteries, blankets, and candles the bus already carries. It is obvious that no one has forgotten the Christmas Storm of 1967.

That particular year, by the day before Christmas, most of the annual events had already taken place. The wreath competition at the garden club was won for the ninth year in a row by Martha Luker. The parade had expanded its route to seven blocks which created confusion with those who did not get the message. And, of course, that was the last year that Beauman's Pond United Methodist Church presented their Singing Tree.

The Singing Tree was a huge structure—almost fifty feet tall—which allowed the Methodist choir to stand in a tree-like shape, one on top of the other. The choir perched on platforms, sticking their heads through pine limbs that had been placed there for authenticity as they sang like live decorations.

During that year's performance, with the entire town in attendance, Haywood Perkins fell from the third tier and almost broke his neck. The Singing Tree was history.

To this day, no one agrees on exactly why the tradition was dumped. The obvious answer is the danger factor, but there are a few people who still blame Miss Edna Thigpen and her editorial in the *Sawyerton Springs Sentinel.* "Is it a good idea," she asked, "to commercialize this season even in our churches? When a man with no record of clumsiness falls from a fake tree while singing 'Here Come Santa Claus' as the minister of the congregation dances down the aisle dressed as the fat man himself . . . is someone trying to tell us something?" And so after a brief discussion of church leaders, the Singing Tree was dismantled for good.

For as long as anyone can remember, the people of Sawyerton Springs have attended a Christmas Eve service at the Baptist and Methodist churches. That particular year, however, on December 23, the Baptists had somehow flooded the sanctuary at Grace Fellowship. It had been blamed on faulty plumbing in the baptistery, but most Methodists smugly assumed it to be just one more piece of evidence that the Lord leaned heavily toward "sprinkling."

Pastor Wade Ward, being a friend of my dad—the Baptist minister—invited our congregation to join his Methodist flock for a combined service. "Really, Larry," Pastor Ward told my father, "it might be good for your people, you know, kind of give them a chance at a second opinion!" In any case, that is how we all came to be packed into the Methodist church that night.

The service itself was different from anything I had ever experienced. Not only was the building unfamiliar and "Holy, Holy, Holy" not the first song in the hymnal—it was the first time in my life that I had been to a church in which my father was not preaching.

Pastor Ward was a great guy. Always quick with a joke, he was one of the most popular men in town. He was then in his mid-thirties, good looking, with a touch of gray already in his hair. "Howbowcha!" he would say when he passed you on the street. "Fine, Pastor," we would answer, and he'd be on his way.

I asked my mom once why everyone called Pastor Ward "Pastor" and they called my dad "Brother." "Isn't Dad a pastor too?" I asked.

"Yes," Mom replied with a smile.

"And what about Pastor Ward," I continued, "I bet he has a brother."

"Right again," she said.

"Then why . . ." I went on like that for about ten more minutes. My mother was a very patient woman.

Altogether the service was wonderful. We sang "O, Little Town of Bethlehem" and "It Came Upon a Midnight Clear." Pastor Ward even asked my father to pray.

The evening was also a success for me personally. Though I was only eight years old at the time, I had already become addicted to making my friends laugh. That night, not only were my usual Baptist targets in attendance—Kevin Perkins, Lee Peyton, and the Luker boys—I had a new audience as well.

The Methodist kids, Dickie Rollins, Steve Krotzer, and the others, were helpless in my grasp. Weird noises during the sermon . . . cow sounds during "Away in a Manger" . . . everything I did worked that night. They literally laughed out loud. From the choir, their parents gave them the "wait 'til I get you home" look as I managed my usual straight face.

The big hit of the night, in my opinion, was my version of "We Three Kings." As the congregation sang the traditional words, I spiced it up a bit. In a voice just loud enough for my friends to hear, I sang:

We three kings of orient are
Tried to smoke a loaded cigar
It went boom and we went zoom
All through the ladies' bathroom.

Dickie, Steve, and the rest of them doubled over the pews as I kept singing—looking for all the world as if I were appalled at their behavior.

As the last carol was sung, the big double doors in the back of the sanctuary were swung open. I will never forget the sight they revealed: Snow. I had never seen it before. Snow—just like on television. White, soft, and covering everything, it was, at the time, the most incredible thing I had ever seen.

No one said a word as we all stood there looking. The trees around Beauman's Pond appeared to be covered with frosting. The cars in the parking lot all looked alike, and the road was not even visible as the snow continued to fall in great swirling sheets.

Finally, from the middle of the group crowded around the door, someone broke the silence. It was Pastor Ward. "Lord," he said, "we are amazed!"

Not to be outdone, I suppose, my father also spoke. "Lord," he said, "we are in awe!"

Then we heard another voice. It was Dr. Peyton. "Lord," he said, "we are stuck!"

It was true. We were snowed in! Now, one must realize that there were only two or three inches on the ground, but to us, it might as well have been two or three feet. Snow in south Alabama is like rain in Los Angeles or grits in New York—an extremely rare occurrence.

Once when I was in the first grade, a teacher thought she saw a flurry. All the kids were packed up and sent home. "A snowstorm is dangerous!" I was told. And now, here we were, everyone in town snowbound together in one building. At least we were in church— God save us all!

"I think I can make it," Tom Henley said. "I can get help." For a moment we stared at him. Then a voice from the back of the room asked, "Who will you call, Tom? We're all here."

Tom thought about that for a bit then said, "I'm going anyway. I'm not spending Christmas here," and with that he trudged into the parking lot. At first, he couldn't find his car. As he brushed the snow from several others, Mr. Wooley yelled to him, "Be sure to clean mine, Tom!" We all laughed.

Finally, he found his Oldsmobile, got it to crank, and after bouncing off four other vehicles, Tom returned to the safety of the church. "We'll never get out of here," he said. "We're doomed."

"Well, I might have gotten through," Miss Luna said, "if you hadn't knocked my truck into the ditch!"

"Next time don't park by the ditch," he replied.

"I wouldn't be here at all," Miss Luna fumed, "if you Methodists hadn't wanted to show off your big church. We should have ignored the invitation. God flooded our sanctuary to warn us! He tried to tell us to stay home!"

"Listen here, you old lady . . ." he said as he started toward her.

"Tom!" a voice rang out. It was Pastor Ward. "None of that now . . . Everyone, please, come back in and settle down."

For a while we all just sat there. *What would people in Minnesota do in this situation*, we wondered. Charles Raymond Floyd began to cry. Maybe because he was scared or maybe because Phillip Wilson told him that Santa Claus would be skipping us this year. I was scared too. Some of the adults began to pick up the argument that Tom and Miss Luna had begun. They bickered about what to do and who got us into this mess in the first place and whether or not anybody had food we could ration. People were nervous, and they were beginning to take it out on each other.

Suddenly, everyone grew silent. Someone was singing.

"Come, they called him, pa rum pa pum pum."

Where was that coming from? We looked at each other.

"A new born King to see, pa rum pa pum pum."

There it was again, a tiny voice, from the corner of the church.

"Our finest gifts to bring, pa rum pa pum pum."

We crept closer to the voice. It was so soft, yet it cut through our tension and irritability like a knife.

"To lay before the King, pa rum pa pum pum, rum pa pum pum, rum pa pum pum."

It was Jill Perkins, Kevin's younger sister, daughter of Haywood and Louise. In the midst of the squabbling and worry, the five-year-old had crawled under a pew and was singing her favorite Christmas carol.

As we gathered around her, Pastor Ward urged, "Keep singing, honey." And she did.

"Come, they called him, pa rum pa pum pum."

Soon, we all joined in. Those who didn't know the words kept the beat with a steady "prrum, prrum, prrum, prrum."

It was a magical moment. People who rarely spoke to each other were smiling and holding hands. I looked at my mother—she had tears in her eyes. Over and over, we sang the song until finally it was quiet. Pastor Ward took a deep breath. "And a little child shall lead them," he said.

"Joy to the world, the Lord is come . . ." someone sang, and everyone joined in. We sang for hours that Christmas Eve, and I remember noticing after a while that it no longer seemed cold. There was a warmth in that place that night that will last a lifetime. It was a flame rekindled by a little girl who reminded us of how much we really love each other, how much we really care.

As I lay my head in my mother's lap and drifted off to sleep, the last thing I heard was my mom and dad singing. Their voices mingled with those of other parents who were also holding their sleeping children.

"Oh, the weather outside is frightful, but *our* fire is so delightful. And since we've no place to go—let it snow, let it snow, let it snow!"

CHAPTER 21

For several hours last week, the whole town was buzzing. It didn't matter who I called, everyone was talking about the same thing. "Did you hear," they would say, "about Billy Pat Williams's midnight walk?" I had indeed, and in fact, it seemed that so had everyone else! Actually, Billy Pat's walk did not occur at midnight. It took place somewhere around two in the morning, but I'm getting ahead of myself.

Billy Pat Williams has lived in Sawyerton Springs for nineteen years, which is not enough time to be considered anything more than a newcomer by some of the older citizens. It is of no significance to some of them that he once served two terms on the county commission or that he and his wife, Ginny, raised three daughters here. Most of them (at least silently) agree with the outspoken opinion of Miss Luna Myers, who once told her Golden Agers Sunday School class, "If you weren't born here, get out."

Another strike against him is his occupation. Billy Pat owns and operates the only Toyota dealership in the tri-county area. One must understand that this in itself verges on original sin among townspeople who drive Fords and Chevrolets almost without exception. Why, you might ask, would someone drive the same kind of car for thirty years? "Because my father did," is the answer, "and his before him. And if you want to drive a foreign car, get out."

It isn't my intention to portray these people as rude or unkind. In fact, quite the opposite is true. There is, however, a set of standards by which one is expected to abide in a small town, and if you don't, well, Atlanta or Birmingham are only a few hours away!

Everyone likes Billy Pat, though. It's obvious in the way he is treated. He is talked about, laughed at, and watched very darn carefully for any wrong move. After all, in Sawyerton Springs, if he wasn't well liked, he'd just be ignored.

Billy Pat, Ginny, and their three daughters have lived in their present home on Keating Drive for four years now. It's the only two story, red-brick, three-bedroom, two-and-one-half-bathroom house in the neighborhood. That in itself would have been enough for a week's worth of gossip, but Billy Pat and Ginny didn't just move into an existing house. They built it.

For weeks and weeks and weeks it went on. "So Billy Pat, I see over on Keating Drive where a wood house ain't good enough for ya." Or "Well, well. Here comes Billy Pat. Maybe we should call you Mr. Billy Pat now that you're building that mansion over on Keating." Rick Carper, who lives down the street, got in the best one. "Say, Billy Pat," he said, "what's a half bathroom? Is that for when you've only got to go a little bit?"

And on it went. Recently after a five-car month at the dealership, Billy Pat considered putting in a pool, but Ginny wouldn't let him do it. "No need to throw our good fortune in someone else's face," she said. Besides, she was close friends with Rebecca Peyton, Lee's wife, and she knew that when they built their pool and had that beautiful fountain installed, they never got use it. Every Friday night it seemed, one or another of the town's teenagers would throw a box of laundry detergent over the fence into the water and what with that fountain . . . well, she was not going to go through that!

The three girls, Bonnie Pat, Janine, and Janelle, are a source of pride for their parents. They're relatively nice looking, have never made below a C on any report card ever, and most important, they don't drink. Billy Pat, however, will admit, if pressed, that Janelle has come in on more than one weekend evening acting kind of goofy.

When Billy Pat feels the need to escape the female environment in which he lives, he'll slip out the back door, whistle for his dog, Barney, and take a walk. Up Keating toward Cherokee, on Cherokee for a bit, a right on Randal, then cut through the Rollins's backyard back to Keating, and home.

Billy Pat loves these times with Barney. Barney never talks back, never asks him to fix anything, never asks why. I ran into them several months back when I was visiting, and as we exchanged pleasantries, I patted Barney's black and white spotted head. "Watch out," Billy Pat warned, "if he bites you, you'll be doomed to eternal Dalmatian!" We both chuckled. It didn't matter that Billy Pat says that every time I pet his dog. He's a nice guy, so I laugh.

As I understand it, Barney was a gift. Not a gift to Billy Pat, but a gift from him. Billy Pat bought the dog from a breeder in Birmingham, and he fully intended to give him as a birthday present to Mike Martin, his best friend. Mike's birthday was still three days away, so Billy Pat had decided to let his family enjoy the pup in the meantime.

Why, he wondered as he drove home with that cute puppy in his lap, *did a man feel some primal urge to give an animal as a present to another man? It was almost as weird as Ginny's compulsion to fix up her unmarried friends with blind dates.* But there he was, heading home with a dog he couldn't give to Mike until Tuesday.

When Billy Pat opened the sliding glass door to the den and put the puppy on the floor, the reaction he observed in Ginny and the girls led him to believe he might have made a mistake. And he had. The pup looked at him slyly as if to say, "Gotcha! You didn't really think you could keep me for awhile and then give me away, did you?" And sure enough, after three days, Mike Martin received a case of shotgun shells, and Barney was Billy Pat's dog.

Wednesday night a week ago, Billy Pat and Ginny crawled into bed about ten-thirty. They were both exhausted. Ginny had spent what felt like a year that day cleaning the house, and Billy Pat was emotionally drained. Serving as chairman of the Grace Fellowship Baptist Church Planning Committee did that to him. Earlier that evening after prayer meeting, he had spent a good solid hour listening to Roger Luker and Miss Luna Myers debate the pros and cons of a covered-dish social versus catering by Cossar's Fried Chicken.

They went to sleep quickly, despite a disagreement over whose night it was to shut off the bathroom light. (Billy Pat's, it turned out.) Everything was quiet until sometime after midnight when Billy Pat was jolted awake by a blood-curdling scream and the words "Help! They're killing him!"

Billy Pat rolled onto the floor carrying the sheets and bedspread with him. He was halfway under the bed when he came fully awake. In the momentary fog, he hadn't been certain whether or not he was the one being killed! Suddenly, he realized that it was Ginny who was screaming, and as he scrambled to untangle himself from the possibility of death by linen, he heard Bonnie Pat, Janine, and Janelle join in the chorus.

Only a few minutes before, Ginny had sleepily gone to the bathroom for a glass of water. Returning to her side of the bed, she paused at the front window and glanced down the street. Noticing movement under the street light, Ginny stared intently and immediately made sense of the motion. It was a dogfight . . . and right in the middle of it was Barney!

By the time Billy Pat made it off the floor and to the window, the three girls were crying and screaming as loud as their mother, who by now was also yelling at Billy Pat. "For heaven's sake, Billy Pat," she shrieked, "do something!"

And so he did. He ran to the front door and bolted outside. Showing an amazing presence of mind usually reserved for veterans of combat or big city paramedics, Billy Pat knew he could not break up the dogfight with his bare hands. On his way off the porch, he grabbed the American flag that always hung from the railing on an eight-foot pole and ran down the street as fast as he could go.

Arriving at the scene of the dogfight, he held the flagpole high over his head and swept the flag into the pack—back and forth. Billy Pat threw a schnauzer into a neighbor's yard. A collie-shepherd mix was knocked off his feet, dogs were flying everywhere. He even hit Barney on the back. The look of surprise on the dogs' faces was evident. It was as if they were saying, "Is that your dad, Barn? What's he doing out here in the middle of the night?"

Though it seemed to Billy Pat that an enormous amount of time had passed, within thirty seconds of joining the hostilities, he stood alone. The dogs, either from a fear of the flagpole or a belief that the bearer of it was insane, had all disappeared. He listened and could hear nothing but his own heavy breathing.

Turning to walk back to his house, Billy Pat froze. Headlights. And they were coming right at him. It was as if Billy Pat Williams woke up again in just that instant, because he had a clear mental image of exactly how he looked: an upstanding member of the community, who just happened to be wearing red satin boxer shorts and carrying an American flag down the middle of the street at two o'clock on a cold, January morning!

As Billy Pat stood there, bathed in the approaching light, he couldn't even come up with a plausible lie about exactly what in the world he was doing. Before he even thought to run, the car pulled up. Naturally, it was Roger Luker, the town's only policeman. For a moment, neither said a word. Then, shining his flashlight from the red satin boxers to Billy Pat's face, Roger cocked an eyebrow and said simply, "Billy Pat?"

"I know you're wondering what I'm doing out here," Billy Pat replied. "I'm breaking up dogfights."

They looked around. Not a dog in sight.

"Billy Pat," Roger said with a smirk on his face, "you're doing a wonderful job."

As Billy Pat watched the tail lights of the patrol car vanish down the street, he knew he had not heard the last of this. And he hasn't. He won't hear the last of it for a very long time. But he doesn't really mind. He thinks it's pretty funny himself, and after all, he lives in a small town—if they didn't like him, nobody would've said a word.

CHAPTER 22

I WAS IN LOVE. HER NAME WAS SHARON HOLBERT, AND SHE was the prettiest girl I had seen in nine years. Her beautiful face, framed by short, dark hair, was covered with freckles, and the flat sandals she wore slapped the ground like firecrackers when she ran. And when she ran, Sharon was faster than any boy in our third-grade class.

The first time I saw her was on the playground. At the time, she was beating Lee Peyton within an inch of his life. She seemed almost elegant—sitting there on his back punching his head. It was at that moment that I knew she would be mine. She was gorgeous.

Around October of that year, I asked a friend of Sharon's to ask Sharon if Sharon would "go" with me. I wasn't really certain what it meant to go with someone, but I had heard that if you went with a person, you couldn't go with someone else. That sounded great to me.

During first recess, her friend popped the question. I watched them talking from across the playground. I saw my emissary point at me as Sharon squinted, trying to get a better look. Actually, I watched this drama unfold upside down.

"You know him, Sharon," her friend seemed to be saying. "He's the one hanging by his knees on the monkey bars. You know . . . the cool one."

Luckily, Sharon told her friend to tell me that yes, she would go with me. The bell rang, and we ran back into class.

Arithmetic held no interest for me that day. Who really cared what ten times three equaled? Not me, that was for sure. Sharon Holbert was all mine. She would walk with only me, be on my team for relay races, and beat up who I asked her to—she was mine.

During lunch, I winked at my woman from across the lunchroom. She turned red. *Love is wonderful*, I thought. Then at second recess, Sharon told her friend to tell me that we were breaking up.

I was crushed. What had gone wrong? We had such a good relationship. All I knew was that the girl of my dreams had been mine for three-and-a-half hours, and I had never actually spoken to her.

Sharon continued to be the object of my love for the next several years. *One day,* I thought, *she will love me too. I will change. I will become the man of her dreams.*

Was I not handsome enough? In the fourth grade I grew sideburns—hair that grew down past my ear lobes, which I kept wet and pointed just like the crew on *Star Trek*. I knew Sharon liked *Star Trek*, and I went to school every day looking just like Captain Kirk.

I also tried to curl the hair on the back of my neck to look more like Bobby Sherman or David Cassidy. I did this by putting my hands behind my head, folding my hair up, and pressing as hard as I could. This process didn't actually curl my hair so much as it made it stick straight out. Another year went by, and unbelievably—as good as I looked—Sharon was not impressed.

Maybe, I thought in the fifth grade, *I don't have the proper family background.* So I told everyone that Elvis Presley was my uncle. I hadn't said anything until now, I explained, because whenever Uncle Elvis came to Sawyerton Springs, he preferred to keep it quiet. "And besides," I told Sharon, "my mother—Joyce Presley Andrews—had asked me not to tell."

Not surprisingly, none of my classmates believed me. In fact, after a few weeks of recounting my adventures with Uncle Elvis, the prevailing attitude seemed to be, "Prove it."

Fortunately for me, Mr. Michael Ted Williams—the town's biggest Elvis fan—had given me a picture of the King for my seventh birthday. I found it stuck between some old comic books. With a ball point pen, I wrote: "To my nephew Andy, who I have a good time doing things with—from your uncle, Elvis."

The next day, Kevin Perkins wanted desperately to believe me (even though he said Elvis wrote like a fifth grader), but the object of the exercise, Sharon, was *not* impressed.

During the sixth grade, I wrote songs. Intending to dazzle her with creativity, I composed masterpieces like "You've Lost That Lovin' Feeling," "Cathy's Clown," "Smoke Gets in Your Eyes," and many more. My parent's record collection was a huge source of inspiration as I put the lyrics on paper.

At this point, I felt I was gaining a little ground. Sharon seemed genuinely interested in me. I was knocking out the hits once or twice every week and passing them to Kevin during English class. He passed them to her during history.

This might have gone on indefinitely had I not seen Sharon in our church one Sunday. Her family was Methodist, but there was Sharon—sitting with her friend Glenda Johnson in the third row—surrounded by Baptists. The next day, wanting to show her that I was as spiritually minded as she, I gave her a new song I had just written. It was to tuck in her Bible, I suggested.

With the hindsight of several decades giving me much clearer vision, I doubt if I would have chosen the same song to "write" for Sharon's Bible. She, of course, recognized the words to "Onward Christian Soldiers," realized that she had been suckered, and was not impressed.

For a long time, Sharon didn't speak to me. I suffered a severe case of writer's block and never wrote another song. Elvis also stopped dropping by about that time. But I still had my sideburns, if not my girl.

The summer of our sixth grade year came and went. Sharon had spent her vacation at camp, so I hadn't seen her for three months. When she returned, she was more beautiful than ever. She was also about a foot and a half taller.

While we had been relatively the same height in May, all of a sudden in September, I was saying, "Hi, Sharon," to her collarbone. She was a giant. Or I was a midget—I wasn't sure which.

Seventh grade was tough enough without this humiliation. It got even worse when Steve Luker asked her to go with him, and she said yes. He asked her himself! He walked right up to Sharon (I was standing there) and over my head said, "Hey. You wanna go with me?"

"I guess," she replied.

"Groovy," he said and strolled away.

That Steve was something else. I was intimidated. For one thing, he was as tall as Sharon, and for another, he was in the eighth grade. He was worldly. He played football and basketball, and he clicked the heels of his shoes by dragging his feet when he walked down the hallway at school.

The "Steve-Sharon matchup" lasted until the first of December. Steve told everyone he broke up with her so he wouldn't have to buy a Christmas present. That made me mad, and I told him so. He pushed me into a bush and laughed.

As February rolled around, I eyed the fourteenth with optimism. That was the day that Grace Fellowship Baptist Church held the annual Valentine's banquet, and as a seventh grader, I was now eligible to attend.

In the hall one afternoon by her locker, I asked Sharon to be my date. "To what?" she asked.

"To the Grace Fellowship Baptist Church Annual Valentine's Banquet," I answered. "What do you say?"

"Well . . ." She hesitated.

I was not going without a date, and this was the only date I wanted. I stepped up the attack: "C'mon, please? We'll have a great time. And besides, I'm dying . . ." I paused to catch my breath and in that moment, I saw Sharon's eyes open wide.

Now understand, after my breath, I was intending to complete my thought—which was something like, "I'm dying to see the Great Gossamer, who is a Christian magician we are having at the banquet." That was my intention.

But as I watched Sharon's eyes fly open and her face go pale, I knew immediately what had happened. And I took advantage of it.

"You . . . you're dying?" Sharon asked in a soft voice.

Looking down at my feet and then up into her incredible tear-filled eyes, I said, "Yes. Yes, I am."

"What's wrong?" she asked.

And in an answer that wasn't exactly a lie, I said, "It's my heart."

The night of the fourteenth, I walked up the sidewalk in front of Sharon's house. I wore black-and-white plaid pants with a red shirt. The cream-colored sport coat matched the hearts on my black-and-cream tie. My belt was white. It complemented my shoes, which were also white with gold buckles on the side. I looked good.

I carried a corsage. My mother, who waited in the car, had coached me on giving it to my date and what to do after the corsage had been presented. At the door, I was perfect.

"Sharon," I gushed, "you are more beautiful than the flowers I brought."

Then I addressed Sharon's mother. "Mrs. Holbert," I said, "will you pin this on her dress? I am so clumsy sometimes. By the way, what time would you like me to have her home?"

Sharon's mother rubbed her mouth with her hand to hide her smile. "About nine-thirty would be fine," she said.

The banquet was memorable. The chicken was broiled, which was not really the way I liked it, but as Sharon pointed out, it was better for my heart. The Great Gossamer truly was great. He made an analogy between sawing a woman in half and the magic of the Lord in our lives.

When it was all over, my mother drove us to get ice cream and then on to Sharon's house. As I walked her to the door, Sharon said, "You aren't really dying, are you?"

"Yes," I answered. "I mean, no. No, I'm not. Not soon anyway."

She smiled. "My mother told me that you weren't. She said you were just trying to get me to like you.

As we reached the door, I was silent. Sharon continued. "You don't have to say that stuff to get me to like you, you know. I always kinda have anyway. Thanks for tonight." And with that, she kissed me and ran inside. I stood there for a few minutes, not believing what I had just experienced. She liked me. She said so right before she kissed me. And it wasn't an ordinary kiss either. It was *right* near the mouth.

I walked back to the car that night a different young man. I carried with me a confidence that can only be given to a young man by a young lady. Through the years, Sharon remained my friend even though we never went with each other or anything close to that. But I'll always remember that Valentine's Day, and I'll always remember what I told my mother as I crawled into the front seat. I shut the door behind me, grinned, and said, "Finally. She was impressed."

SPRING

CHAPTER 23

NORMAN'S GROCETERIA WAS BUSIER THAN USUAL THIS past week. Every item in the store had been marked down. Ladies crowded the aisles, browsing more than anything, sipping complimentary coffee, and talking among themselves.

By Thursday afternoon, even some of the men in town had wandered in to see if what they'd heard was true. And, after looking around a bit, they all met at the meat cooler and agreed. Yes, it seemed, Norman had priced every single item exactly three cents cheaper than Rick's Rolling Store.

Dick Rollins was holding a frozen chicken that had an X slashed over the $2.19 sticker. In red Magic Marker, it was now priced $2.16. "What'n heck started this whole thing?" he asked.

"You got me," George Cossar answered. "You know Norman!" The group of men smiled and nodded.

"Oh, yeah," Tom Henley said, grinning, "we know Norman!"

Walking toward the entrance, George put his arm around Kevin Perkins's shoulder, opened his eyes real wide, and said, "Here we go again!"

Norman Green was born in Sawyerton Springs, but his family moved to Birmingham when he was eight. That in itself explains much of the town's reaction to Norman. "He is from here; therefore, he is one of us. But living 'up North' sure did give him a lot of weird ideas!"

Norman came back to the Springs after college and worked for several years at Henley's Hardware. By all accounts, he was a successful employee. The men in town enjoyed talking to him about hunting or fishing, and consequently, they would stop in most afternoons.

Norman was especially knowledgeable about catfish, and by selling them to restaurants in nearby Foley, he made quite a bit of extra money. Every morning, he would rise before daylight to check his trotlines. Walking a good seven or eight miles in the dark between streams and ponds was nothing for Norman. He'd make it to work by seven o'clock in the morning stay until 6 o'clock in the evening, and run his trotlines again after dark.

Day after day, every single day, Norman kept up that schedule. On Sundays, when Tom closed the hardware store, Norman went to church, and in the afternoon, he prepared his lines for the following week. No one worked harder than Norman Green.

"What's the deal?" people would ask. "He's gonna work himself to death before he's thirty!" But before too long, Norman's motives became apparent. He had a dream. He was not content to live out his life working for someone else—Norman wanted his own business.

He saved every penny that wasn't needed for immediate living expenses and within a few years had quite a nest egg. It helped that Norman lived modestly and was extremely frugal. Or as his friends put it . . . cheap.

Kevin and George were in the car behind Norman one day when Norman suddenly put on the brakes, hopped out, and picked up an aluminum can he had seen beside the road. "Geez! Get a load of this, would ya," Kevin said laughing. Norman held up the can and smiled, waving as he climbed back in his car.

"That Norman is tighter'n paint on a wall," Kevin said. "When he blinks, his kneecaps move."

George chuckled and shook his head. "I don't know," he said. "A guy working that hard? He'll probably own the town one day."

Well, Norman didn't want the town, but he did intend to have a piece of it. His ideas were endless and some of them had a few folks worried. For a time, he talked about opening a catfish restaurant. He was going to call it Norman's Cat House. That particular choice of names didn't go over well at the Baptist church.

"I'll put a big sign out on the bypass," Norman told Dick one morning. "It'll say, FOR A GOOD TIME, COME TO NORMAN'S CAT HOUSE . . . DOWNTOWN SAWYERTON SPRINGS! Then out to the side I'll put, CHILDREN—HALF PRICE."

Dick rolled his eyes. "Oh, brother," he said. "Here we go again."

Those four words, "here we go again," are used quite often by whoever happens to be discussing Norman at the time. His ideas have given him the reputation of one who is not so grounded as a person should be. "Or maybe," Kevin says, "he's just so far ahead of the rest of us."

For more than a year, all Norman talked about was his vision for a new chain of Jell-O stores. "They won't sell nothing but Jell-O," he'd explain. "This is an idea whose time has come! I mean, everybody knows where to go for a burger. Pizza places are everywhere, and right here in town we got Cossar's for fried chicken. So you tell me," he'd always ask smugly, "where do you go for a good bowl of Jell-O?"

Norman really had the whole thing planned out. He had drawings of what his stores would look like. He even had a menu printed that offered a variety of flavors: lime, cherry, orange, strawberry, and "specialty fruit cocktail." "The price will be the best thing," Norman said. "Fifty cents a bowl, a quarter a square, or a nickel per cube. That way even kids can come by after school and buy a dime's worth."

"And another thing," Norman would continue, "we will only serve fresh Jell-O. Our motto will be 'If It Ain't Wiggling—We Ain't Got It!' I'll advertise the phone number so that people can call before they drive over. They'll call and ask, 'Is the Jell-O hard yet?'"

Gradually, this particular obsession of Norman's wore off. He had planned to name the chain of restaurants Jiggles and insisted that the world was ready for such a place. It became obvious, however, that Sawyerton Springs was not.

Some folks, including Miss Edna Thigpen at the *Sentinel,* felt that the name Jiggles was suggestive and that a hangout of that sort could only lead to immorality. So when pressure came to bear, Norman backed off.

"But don't tell me it won't work," he said for weeks. "Don't even try to tell me that. It's a great idea, and someone, somewhere, will make millions with it. Everybody thought Einstein was a nut case, too!"

Now understand, no one really thinks Norman is a nut case. It's just that his ideas always seem to represent an uncomfortable change. That's why everyone was surprised when he decided to open a grocery store. It was, well . . . ordinary. The town needed a grocery store, that was a fact. Until Rick's Rolling Store began operations in 1986, people drove all the way to Foley for groceries.

Rick's Rolling Store, actually an old school bus converted into a supermarket on wheels, literally changed the way people shopped. Suddenly, the store was at your door, allowing you the opportunity to shop conveniently.

The only catch to shopping with Rick was the selection. There's not much room on a bus—even with the added shelves and hooks—therefore, people pretty much took what they could get. It wasn't like there was a choice of frozen beans, fresh beans, dried beans, or canned beans. It was just plain beans, and a person felt lucky that he didn't have to drive twenty miles to get them.

Norman's grand opening was on a Saturday in August eight years ago. He had NORMAN'S GROCETERIA written in huge letters over the front entrance, which faced College Avenue. He called it groceteria because he said, "It will not only be a grocery store, it will be a cafeteria!"

Tom Henley smiled every time he said the word *groceteria.* "I knew Norman wouldn't open some regular store," he told his wife. "It's not in his nature. I saw GROCETERIA going up on that building, and I said to myself, *here we go again.*"

Well, everything was fine for years. People enjoyed the variety of Norman's, but they still appreciated the convenience of Rick's. Rick and Sue, despite the competition, never resented the groceteria, and in fact, they ate lunch there on Mondays and Thursdays. Norman, as a professional courtesy, never charged for their meals.

Norman kept the steamer in the middle aisle, filled with the special of the day. Dessert was, of course, always Jell-O. As people filed past, they were reminded by Norman's hand-lettered sign to TAKE ALL YOU WANT—EAT ALL YOU TAKE! And they did, until last Monday.

No one showed up. No one. Not even Rick and Sue. As Norman shoveled the turkey tetrazini into freezer bags, he wondered if he'd missed something. "Was there a Rotary luncheon today or what?" he asked aloud to no one in particular. "People are buying groceries, isn't anybody eating lunch?"

Walking home after closing, Norman was still in a quandary. *Why,* he wondered, *would his noon business all of a sudden disappear?* He kicked at a piece of paper that blew across the sidewalk. Seeing the word *store* printed on the front, he picked it up. It was a business flyer.

"Are you tired of the same old lunch? Starting Monday, you can have the food you deserve delivered right to your home or office. Rick's Rolling Store provides you with the same convenience you've enjoyed for years . . . now in our new busateria service!"

Well, had Norman been indoors, he would have hit the roof. He was that mad. His face darkened, his eyes narrowed, and had he not consciously remembered to breathe, he might have suffocated on the spot.

"Traitors," he muttered. He walked fast, and no longer heading home, talked to himself. "No right. They've got no right. I don't sell cloth and buttons and hammers and junk. They've got no right to serve food! Eight years I fed those people. Twice a week for eight years." Norman was boiling now. "That's more than eight hundred meals apiece!"

What really got to Norman was the line about the busateria service! The way he saw it, Rick had stolen his idea. "Groceteria, busateria," Norman said to Miss Edna Thigpen, "it's too close for coincidence. Don't tell me the man thought of it himself!"

Norman had walked straight to Miss Edna Thigpen's house on Keating Drive and was now sitting in her living room. Miss Edna, the owner and editor of the *Sawyerton Springs Sentinel*, was about to make the biggest advertising sale in the history of the newspaper.

"I've got Rick's price list at home," Norman said. "I'll bring it over tomorrow. I want a full-page ad. On the top left, have it say "Rick's Prices" and list every single item in a column underneath. At the top right in big letters, I want "NORMAN'S PRICES!" Underneath, I want each corresponding item marked three cents less.

Norman paid Miss Edna for the ad right there. But before he stalked out of her house, he included one final item. "At the bottom of the page in the biggest letters of all," he directed, "put this: 'CALL FOR OUR NEW LUNCH DELIVERY!'"

When the *Sentinel* came out, Rick knew that he was at war, but after all, he had fired the first shot. Rick lowered his prices. Norman lowered his. Then Rick again. Then Norman. Soon they were giving things away. There's no telling where the whole thing might have gone had it not been for Sue.

Just yesterday, she hauled Rick to Norman's. She got Norman out of his office, and in front of everyone, she said, "You're both acting like kids. You're killing each other off, and the town is laughing at us. I am no longer participating in this fiasco. Rick, I don't know where you'll get your meals for the bus to deliver, but I'm not cooking them! I hate to cook. Why do you think I've eaten at Norman's for eight years?"

Rick started to say something, but withering him with a look, Sue continued. "So this is what we're going to do," she said. "Rick, we will still deliver lunches to anyone in town who wants them. Norman, they will be your lunches. That way, you will both increase your business, and I don't have to cook. Everybody wins. You've been friends too long to let something this stupid come between you."

For a moment, there was silence. Then, slowly, the two men looked at each other and smiled. "That's a great idea," Norman said. "Rick, I don't know why we didn't think of this years ago. We could expand this same concept into other towns. Maybe get a fleet of buses to deliver with. Can you put a refrigerator on one of those things? Jell-O has to be cool, you know. And something else we can try . . ."

As he listened to Norman, Rick put his arm around Sue, gave her a squeeze, and in her ear he whispered, "Here we go again!"

CHAPTER 24

NEVER IN MY LIFE HAD I ENCOUNTERED SUCH BEAUTY. HER perfect face, framed by long, blond hair, featured the most incredible green eyes I had ever seen. Her voice was a symphony and her movements . . . hypnotic.

"Linda Gail," I wanted to say, "I love you. You were meant to be mine." And then I would kiss her. And not just anywhere either. I would kiss her—on the mouth!

Faintly, I thought, I could hear giggling. "Andy? Andy!" Looking up, I saw that wonderful face. She looked worried.

I said, "What's wrong, Linda Gail?"

There was a brief moment of silence. Suddenly, all around me, an entire classroom erupted in laughter. Kevin Perkins, at the desk across the aisle, was slapping Lee Peyton on the back. Steve Krotzer, usually quiet and studious, was practically crying.

I was horrified. Had I just said something? I couldn't remember. Sharon Holbert and Dickie Rollins were howling, Charles Raymond was beating his desk, and Miss Wheeler was standing in the middle of it all with an open English book, looking right at me.

It was about that time when it hit me. I had called Miss Wheeler by her first name. Miss Wheeler was an adult. Miss Wheeler was my third-grade teacher!

"Class!" she said loudly. "Class, calm down!" Pow! She slammed the English book to the floor. Startled into silence, we looked up at her. "I said 'calm down'," she ordered. And then, leaning down to me, she continued, "I'll see you after school."

When the final bell rang, I ducked my head and sat still as my friends left the room. I could hear them laughing in the hall as Lee Peyton did impressions of me. "What's wrong, Linda Gail? What's wrong, Linda Gail?" I wanted to hit him in the stomach.

Miss Wheeler rose from her desk. Closing the door, she walked toward me. "Andy," she began, "I think you're a wonderful young man."

Hey, hey, hey! I thought.

"But," she continued, "If I am to maintain control of the class, you must not call me by my first name. It seems disrespectful."

I stared at her. I didn't really understand what she was saying.

"Do you understand what I am saying?" she asked.

"Yes, ma'am," I answered.

"I know that you didn't intend to be rude," she said, "but let's be careful, okay?" And with that, she put her hand on my shoulder and said, "You are one of my favorites."

I put my hand up on her shoulder and said, "You're one of my favorites too." Then I winked.

Walking home, I smiled as I thought of Miss Wheeler. I could tell she liked me by the way she looked at me after I winked—kind of open mouthed, blinking her eyes. So I had winked again and walked out.

Sawyerton Springs Elementary had two third-grade teachers. One was Miss Wheeler, who was well liked and beautiful. The other was Mrs. Trotter.

Mrs. Trotter was short and wide. She wasn't fat—she was wide. Her eyes bulged and her red hair extended straight up from her flat forehead like fire. Mrs. Trotter waddled around the schoolyard looking for all the world like some demented troll screeching at kids. In fact, that is what we called her: Trotter the Troll.

All through the second grade, we prayed to God in heaven above to reach down his mighty hand and place us in Miss Wheeler's third-grade class. "In thy merciful goodness, spare us, O Lord, from Trotter the Troll." Once I even prayed that at the dinner table. My mother didn't think it was funny, but my dad actually squirted iced tea out his nose.

Third grade with Miss Wheeler was wonderful. Every day, after arithmetic, she would introduce "show and tell," and because we participated alphabetically, I was always first.

As I remember, that was a good year for me. I scored big with baby rat, a picture of Elvis, and a pair of my grandmother's underwear. They were enormous.

Normally for show and tell, one would merely produce something from a sack, but occasionally we would get permission to go into the hall and get our presentation ready. Such was the case on that particular day, and so with Kevin Perkins as my assistant, I retired to the hall. Moments later, we entered the room, each of us through a leg of those massive panties. Miss Wheeler turned a bright red, but to her credit, she never said a word.

As we returned to the hall, we were triumphant and smug in our obvious victory. Often we were outclassed by whatever Lee Peyton brought from his father's doctor's office. Leaning against the lockers, I was about to help Kevin out of the right leg when the door adjacent to us opened. It was Mrs. Trotter.

She came fully to the middle of the hall before she saw us. Stopping suddenly, she looked, turning her head as if to adjust her vision, and then with a croaking noise not at all unlike a giant toad, she came for us.

In an instant, both Kevin and I knew she was not coming *to* us—she was coming *for* us. So we ran. We ran down the hall as fast as we could go with Mrs. Trotter close behind. It was as if we had stolen *her* underwear, and she was determined to get them back. "O Lord," Kevin said, "save us from Trotter the Troll!"

We ran outside, across the playground, and back into the other end of the school building. It was like a two-man sack race. Kevin would fall, and I would fall. I would fall, and Kevin would fall. We were so scared that simply getting out of the underwear never occurred to us.

Shortly, we were back where we started. Opening the door to Miss Wheeler's room, we fell inside and shut it behind us. Mrs. Trotter, seeing where we had gone, was running for the open door just as it closed. Boom! She hit it like a linebacker. As we looked up at the small window in the door, her bulging eyes rolled back in her head, and Trotter the Troll slowly slid out of sight.

I found out later that Miss Wheeler had explained everything to the principal and smoothed things over with Mrs. Trotter. We never got in trouble, my parents never knew, and I was more positive than ever that Miss Wheeler was the greatest teacher in the world.

As the years passed, Miss Wheeler came through for us all many times. She remained a friend even when I wasn't in her class, but because her ultimate goal was to teach high school English, I was fortunate enough to be her student twice more as she taught different grades.

The next time I caught up with Miss Wheeler was in a seventh-grade English and literature class. The assignment one week was "poetry parodies." Using poems from our literature book, we were to "make the verse our own" while maintaining the style of the original. The poems were to remain recognizable—humor was encouraged.

Still trying to impress Miss Wheeler, I chose the longest poem in the book and made a mess out of "The Wreck of the Hesperus." Lee Peyton did the best job, I thought, with his stunning adaptation of the Joyce Kilmer classic, "Trees."

> *I think that I shall never know*
> *A poem so lovely as my toe.*
> *A toe that may in summer wear*
> *Scabs from stumps everywhere.*

As the years passed, my crush on Miss Wheeler developed into an admiration for her abilities as a teacher. Her classes were taught in an atmosphere of laughter and excitement, yet she demanded respect. The day after Lee received an A for "Toes," she paddled him for calling her "Wheeler Dealer."

I was thrilled to be assigned to Miss Wheeler's English class as a senior. It was good to see that she had not changed. Our first- period discussions often carried over into second period study hall, which she also supervised. Most of our class had signed up for study hall during that time, and to this day, a majority of my high school memories revolve around Miss Wheeler and those first two periods.

We talked, argued, laughed, and teased her about Coach Rainsberger, who the year before had taken her to our junior-senior prom wearing gym shoes with his tuxedo. I suppose, however, that there came a time when, due to familiarity, we began to see ourselves as Miss Wheeler's equal. This was not an accurate perception.

We had mistaken her interest and concern for us as an inability to see through mischief. We could have saved ourselves a zero on a major test if we'd only listened when Miss Wheeler said, "Remember, to take advantage is to invite trouble."

It was a crisp March morning—not cold, but crisp. Kevin, Lee, Dickie, and I had gotten onto Beauman's Pond at daylight. We were fishing before school. The day had already been fantastic. Kevin and Dickie had their limit on bass; Lee and I were one shy.

The problem we saw, as we stopped to discuss it, was time. In less than thirty minutes, first period would begin. None of us had ever gotten a limit before and now here was a chance for all of us to accomplish that feat. But if we stayed for a limit, Dickie pointed out, we'd be late for school. And today, he warned, was the midterm exam.

"Big deal," Kevin said. "We'll just tell Miss Wheeler we had a flat tire. You know she'll believe us. Then we can make up the test during study hall.

So that's what we did. Confidently, we strode into Miss Wheeler's room just as the second period bell rang. Looking up from her desk, she asked, "Where were you?"

"We had a flat tire on my car, Miss Wheeler," Lee said. "We were down near Henley's Hardware on the back street."

She glanced at me. I nodded.

Kevin spoke. "We tried to hurry in time for the test, Miss Wheeler, but we just couldn't make it."

She glanced at me. I nodded.

"We're ready to take the test, Miss Wheeler," Dickie said. "We'll make it up right now. We'll make it up right here in study hall."

She glanced at me. I nodded.

"Okay," she agreed. "If you're ready to take the test now, let's get to it."

We tried to hide our smiles as we turned to go to our seats.

"I don't want you to sit in your regular places," Miss Wheeler said, "I would like you each to choose one corner of the room."

As we settled into our desks, pen and paper at the ready, the greatest teacher I ever had continued. "Your makeup exam will be all essay," she said. "The essay will be the answer to only one question. And the question is . . ." She paused. "The question is . . . Which tire was flat?"

CHAPTER 25

THE BIG ANNUAL CHAMBER OF COMMERCE DANCE LAST Saturday night was a huge success. Rebecca Peyton and Glenda Perkins headed up the women's committee, which raised enough money to bring in a professional band all the way from North Carolina.

The group, Carl Benson's Wildcats, usually plays high school reunions in the Raleigh area, but Rebecca, having seen them on a local television show, was determined to book them for this year's event. At first everyone had been disappointed because Carl was sick and didn't make the trip. Carl's mother, however, was a "more than ample" substitute on the saxophone.

Everyone in town was there. After all, the Big Annual Chamber of Commerce Dance is the social event of the year. This is the chance to see and be seen. It is also the starting point for a world of gossip. "Isn't that the same powder-blue tux that Dick Rollins wore in his son's wedding last year? Seems kind of a sleazy color. I thought so then, and I think so now. He looks like the doorman in a strip joint."

"What's with Betty Jo and that new necklace? George took

her to Orlando in July, and they're going to New Orleans before Thanksgiving. I don't care what anybody says, they're getting money from somewhere besides that chicken stand!"

Even Lee Peyton was not immune to the rumor mill. Being a doctor, he is watched closely, and though he only had one glass of wine all night, by noon the next day, everyone had heard that he'd been "drunker'n Cooter Brown."

Tom and Terri Henley, Rick and Sue Carper, Roger and Carol Luker were all there and had a wonderful time. The only damper on the evening came during the hour that Miss Edna Thigpen and Miss Luna Myers made their appearances. Because every breath a person takes ends up in the *Sentinel*, people were simply too nervous to have fun.

Billy Pat and Ginny Williams arrived late and left early; Billy Pat has been putting in a lot of hours down at the dealership, and he came home Saturday with a migraine. Ginny had her heart set on the dance, though, so he went and gamely stayed as long as he could. It was about the fourth time Carl Benson's mother did an encore on the same song that Billy Pat decided he'd had all he could take. "'Hunk-A-Hunk-A-Burnin' Love'," he said, "just isn't the same on a saxophone!"

On the way home, they didn't really talk much. Ginny wasn't mad, it was just that she'd looked forward to spending the evening out. In Sawyerton Springs, it isn't every night—or even every Saturday night—when there is something to do.

As they pulled into their driveway, she noticed that Miss Edna and Miss Luna in the house across the street were already home.

Having the two older ladies so close, Ginny figured, could be considered both good and bad. And actually, the good part and the bad part were one and the same.

That, of course, has to do with the fact that Miss Edna and Miss Luna never miss anything. Ever. On the one hand, that is a plus. Keating Drive doesn't need a watchdog. But on the other hand, it can be nuisance. If something (anything) doesn't seem right to them, they never hesitate to call.

The phone will ring.

"Ginny?"

"Yes, Miss Edna," Ginny will sigh.

"Ginny, it's certainly none of my concern, but there is a boy outside cutting your bushes, and I thought you should be aware of it."

"Yes, ma'am," Ginny will respond, "we know. Billy Pat's paying him to do it."

Or one of them might catch Billy Pat at church.

"Billy Pat?"

"Yes, Miss Luna?"

"I couldn't help but notice the amount of your tithe check as your offering plate passed me today. I'm overjoyed your business is doing so well!"

In any case, both of them are eighty-three years old. And as Billy Pat and Ginny keep reminding themselves, "It's just a blessing they're still with us."

Heading in through the front door, Billy Pat almost tripped over the broom he'd left on the porch earlier that day. He cussed, kicked it, and left it there. Once inside, he got out of his suit, fed their dog Barney, and after taking two Sominex tablets and several aspirin, crawled into bed.

Ginny, trying her best to keep out of his way, stayed up and watched the late show—G-Men, starring James Cagney. It was well after midnight when she put on her long, flannel nightgown and eased under the covers beside Billy Pat. He was sleeping soundly, she noted with some relief, and within minutes, Ginny was asleep as well.

Until 2:13 A.M., the only sound in the Williams's house was Billy Pat's quiet snoring and the occasional squeaking noise as Barney shifted positions on the foot of the bed. At 2:14, however, shattering the silence like a bullwhip, the phone rang.

Instinctively, Ginny made a grab at the sound and turned over the glass of water on her night table. "Hello," she answered groggily as she finally found the receiver. "Yes, Miss Luna." Billy Pat groaned. Suddenly, Ginny kicked the covers off and turned on the lamp. "Stay in your room, Miss Luna. We'll be right over!"

"Get up, Billy Pat," Ginny said loudly as she punched him in the back. "Miss Luna says something's in their house!"

Billy Pat was still half asleep, and the combination of Sominex and his wife's fist had him thoroughly confused. "What's in their house?" he asked.

"Something! Just something, Billy Pat. Get up, NOW!" Ginny was already at the bedroom door.

As Billy Pat rolled out of bed and fumbled for his pants, Ginny yelled, "NO TIME!" and pushed her bathrobe into his arms. It was bright pink with yellow flowers, and as he struggled to put it on, she herded him out the front door.

Reaching the yard, Billy Pat stopped. "Now hold on, daggummit," he said. "Just what the heck are we walking into here? Exactly what is 'something'? Are we talking about an escapee from the crazy house, an ax murderer, or just your ordinary gang of killers?"

"Go," Ginny said, "and be careful. I'll call the police." And with that, she pulled the broom off the porch and put it in his hands.

"Oh, great," Billy Pat muttered to himself as he crossed the street, "this'll be a big help."

There was one more thing on Billy Pat's mind at that moment. He had taken a lot of teasing only a few months before when he was seen breaking up a dogfight in the middle of the night. At the time, he was wearing his boxer shorts and wielding an American flag. Ginny's bathrobe and this broom, he knew, would not help his image.

Entering through the side door with the key under the mat, Billy Pat went directly to the bedroom. Miss Edna and Miss Luna, their hair done up in curlers, were cowering in fright between the twin beds. Over and over, they pointed down the hall and stammered, "The den. Something's in the den."

The door to the den was slightly ajar. Peering into the spacious room, Billy Pat noticed the lamp that had been left on in the corner. Its glow allowed him to see almost everything. In fact, the only area he could not see was behind the big sofa that faced him. That,

Billy Pat reasoned, was the only place someone might be hiding.

Billy Pat cleared his throat. He stamped his foot. Nothing. "All right," he said in a loud voice, "I see you. Come on out." He desperately hoped no one would. No one did.

Over his shoulder he shouted, "Johnny! Frank! We're not getting any cooperation—looks like we'll have to bring in the Dobermans!" He waited.

Relatively convinced that no one was behind the sofa, Billy Pat eased into the den. Suddenly, without warning from the right side of the room, the "something" appeared in Billy Pat's face. Instinctively, he ducked and swung the broom, knocking Miss Luna's bowling trophies off the television set.

"It's a flying squirrel," he howled as he swung again. "It's a dang flying squirrel!" Now Billy Pat was mad. All the stress of the past few minutes—feeling as though he might be gunned down any second, not to mention the lack of sleep—he was going to take it out on the squirrel.

As Billy Pat chased the animal around the den, he continued to shout, "It's a flying squirrel," trying to let Miss Edna and Miss Luna know that they had nothing to fear. It didn't work. Evidently, both ladies have an acute phobia that is directly related to rodents, and as far as they were concerned, this was just a rat with wings.

They entered the den screaming at the top of their lungs, "Kill it, Billy Pat! Help! Oh, Lord! Help! Kill it!"

Billy Pat was trying. He broke the light fixture on the ceiling with a backswing, and as the terrified creature scampered across the coffee table, he cleared that piece of furniture with one mighty blow. He missed the squirrel, but an old candy jar, several pictures of relatives, and a miniature gong all ended up on the floor.

At some point during all this ruckus, Miss Luna gave Billy Pat the old .22 rifle she keeps in her closet. "It is already loaded," she said. "Use it and save us all!"

Though Billy Pat had the gun in his hands, it wasn't his intention to actually fire it. When the squirrel came at them again, however, and the hysterical ladies yelled, "SHOOT," he did.

POW! He hit the lamp in the corner. "Shoot, Billy Pat, shoot!" POW! POW! Feathers flew everywhere as two sofa pillows bit the dust. "Help! Kill it, Billy Pat! Help! Shoot! Shoot!" POW, POW, POW, POW, POW!

Between the panic stricken women and the sound of his own shots, Billy Pat had lost all control. When the squirrel ran along a curtain rod, he splintered the pine board paneling above it and put three holes in the window, but the rifle at last was empty.

Before Roger and the squad car arrived, the flying squirrel had sailed through the window Billy Pat had blown out and into the night. He was not harmed and probably told his family a better story than the one Sawyerton Springs is talking about.

And are they ever talking about it! When the *Sentinel* came out yesterday, Billy Pat was fairly certain the town would forget the dogfight. There on the front page was the story of THE SHOOT-OUT ON KEATING DRIVE, complete with an artist's rendering of Billy Pat in the bathrobe—rifle in one hand, broom in the other. The caption read: "Go Ahead, Squirrel. Make My Day."

CHAPTER 26

DICK ROLLINS WAS CLEANING OUT THE FILES IN THE BACK room of his gas station last week. In an old cigar box, he found a ticket for a suit his father had left to be altered at Benson's Department Store in Foley. The ticket was dated May 22, 1959.

The ticket had not been stamped, signifying receipt, so Dick assumed that his father had simply forgotten to pick up the suit. Dick grinned.

He was still grinning later that day as he presented the ticket to Roy Benson in the men's department. "Need to pick up this suit, Roy," Dick said. "We were having the cuffs and sleeves let out."

Roy took the ticket, glanced at it, and went behind the counter. After only a few minutes of poking through files of his own, Roy produced a piece of paper, stared at it a moment, and said, "Dick, those alterations won't be ready until next Thursday."

The people of Sawyerton Springs have shopped in Benson's Department Store since 1931. Located in Foley, it was started during the Depression by Able Benson, and it has remained a family business all these years. After Able's death in 1969, his son and daughter-in-law, Roy and Kaye, kept the place going.

Benson's is by far the biggest building in Foley. It is a three-story, red-brick structure that takes up most of a city block. Huge windows surround the first floor, and Kaye keeps them filled with the latest fashions from Birmingham and Memphis.

April is a busy month at Benson's. The "Summer Soon Sale" is in progress, and the outdoor department picks up with the advent of warm weather and fishing.

Most children from the Springs only visit the department store three times a year—once for school clothes, once for summer clothes, and once at Christmas to see the "Santa's Workshop" window exhibit and experience a brief visit with Santa Claus himself.

The Christmas visit was the only one I ever enjoyed, because it was the only one for which I was not required to try on clothes. I hated shopping with my mother. As if the long drive to Foley wasn't bad enough, it always took us at least an hour to get through Housewares and Home Furnishings on the first floor and Ladies Wear and Shoes on the second floor before we ever saw Boys on the third.

Kaye was a childhood friend of my mother's, so she usually waited on us in the boys' department. I stood around while she and my mother made small talk, after which they picked out what they wanted me to wear. Of course, this was the same every six months—two pairs of jeans, one pair of dress pants, five shirts, four pairs of socks, a pair of dress shoes, and a pair of sneakers.

As I tried them on, looking somewhat newer but more or less the same as I did six months earlier, Kaye would point at me and say, "Fabulous, Fabulous! You just look precious!" My mother would smile and say things like, "He's an eight-and-a-half right now, and he's only in the second grade. He's going to be a big man." Kaye would point at her and say, "That's exactly right!"

The other reason I hated going to Foley was Dr. Paul, our dentist. Since Foley was so far away, my mother always killed two birds with one stone and scheduled my six-month checkup on the same day we went for clothes. As badly as I hated shopping, nothing compared with my dislike for the dentist.

It wasn't that Dr. Paul wasn't an okay guy, it was just that dentists in general scared me to death. And it never helped my attitude that all the adults in town referred to him in less than glowing terms. "Bloody Marcus" was one I heard more than once. I was too young to realize that their animosity toward Dr. Paul had nothing to do with his dental ability—he had hurt their feelings.

Our town has never had its own dentist. Therefore, when Marcus Paul, who was born and reared in Sawyerton Springs, finished dental school at the University of Alabama, everyone assumed that he would open an office in his own hometown. He didn't, and they never forgave him.

Dr. Rudolph Posey, who had been the dentist in Foley for forty-five years, retired and sold his practice to Marcus, building and all. "For gosh sakes," people said, "we have a mortician here, but no dentist!'

Mike Martin, the mortician, agreed. "You're right," he said. "It's a crazy thing. I see a lot of mouths that've been dead longer that their owners." I, for one, did not want a dead mouth, but that is the *only* reason I crawled into that dentist chair every six months.

When Dr. Paul entered the examining room on the day I am about to describe, he was smiling. Dr. Paul was always smiling, which I thought was a good thing for a dentist to do—it showed me that the man could at least take care of his own teeth. He was about five feet ten, in his mid-thirties, and prematurely balding and gray, probably as a result of treating patients like me.

"Hey, buddy," he said, even though I did not feel like his buddy. "You been eating lots of candy? I need the business, you know!" This was Dr. Paul's idea of a joke, and I heard it every time I saw him.

"Ha, ha, ha." I laughed nervously. "Do I have any cavities?"

"Well," he said, "let me look in your mouth. That's the easiest way for me to tell, you know."

"I know," I said.

Sitting down beside me, he grabbed what looked like a curved ice pick, and then he said, "Of course, you don't have to open your mouth, I could go through your nose."

I opened my mouth as wide as I could. My nose, like my feet, was proportionately larger than the rest of me, and I wasn't sure if he was kidding or not.

As he pushed and pulled on my teeth, he quietly talked to Reita, his wife and assistant, who made notes on a pad. "We're missing a molar," he told her at one point, "and I think we need to be missing another one. This joker will have to be extracted." She made a note.

I was concerned. As a second grader, "extract" was not a word with which I was familiar. Although he had both hands and an ice pick in my mouth, I said, "Whmahstakmen?"

"I'm sorry," he said as he placed the ice pick on a table. "Did I hurt you?"

"No, sir," I said. "What does extract mean?"

"It means that we have to make room for one of your permanent teeth."

"Oh. So what does extract mean?" I asked again.

"Pull. Extract means 'to pull.' We have to . . ."

I was already out of the chair. Unfortunately, I was so scared that I had gotten out on the wrong side. Dr. Paul and his wife were now blocking the door. "No," I said as I backed into the corner. "No. No. No!"

Lee Peyton had told me about having his tooth pulled only a month before, and it had sounded horrible. Dr. Paul had used the claw of a hammer to hold down Lee's bottom jaw. Then with another hammer, he had cracked the tooth with several swings and pulled out the pieces with a pair of pliers. There had been blood everywhere, but Lee had never cried. He swore it had happened just like that, and now Bloody Marcus was after me!

I was only a kid, but this was not going to happen. "Please," I said, "stay away." I jerked a mirror off the table and brandished it like a weapon. I had seen the ice pick right beside it, but even in a state of overwhelming panic, I knew my dad would spank me for holding an ice pick on the only dentist in the county.

"Hey, buddy," Dr. Paul said soothingly, "don't worry. This is not going to hurt at all. Honest. You won't feel a thing."

"Really?" I asked. My bottom lip was quivering, and I desperately wanted to believe him. At that point, I almost put down the mirror. Maybe Lee had been lying. Maybe it wouldn't be so bad after all. "You promise I won't feel anything?"

"I promise you won't feel anything," he said. I relaxed for a moment, but then he made a mistake. He added, "You won't feel anything, because first, we are going to knock you out!"

That did it. I yelled as loud as I could, "Ahhhhh! Stay away!"

My God! The man was going to hit me in the head with the hammer before he ever started on my mouth—and with my own mother in the waiting room. "Ahhhhh!" I yelled again. "Stay away!"

Quickly, I lunged for the automatic water gun (still not wanting to risk the ice pick) and sprayed Dr. Paul right in the face. This was an act that my mother personally witnessed, the commotion having drawn her into the battle. It was not her fight, however, and she should not have tried to take part, but she did, so I sprayed her too—an act I immediately recognized as an error on my part.

At that point, I was left alone in the corner with my water gun and mirror. About fifteen minutes later, the end of this story walked into the room in the form of my father. He had been located in the lawn and garden department of Benson's and did not appear to be very happy.

He looked at me for a moment as if I had lost my mind (which, indeed for a while there, I had). Then he pointed at me and said that if I sprayed him I would get a whipping right in front of everybody and that he did not mean maybe. He practically slam-dunked me into the chair, put a mask on my face, punched a button, and left. "Breathe," was the last thing he said.

The next thing I knew, we were in the car driving home. My jaw felt numb, but I didn't remember anything. The extraction actually *had* been painless.

Another good point was that while I had been in Dr. Paul's "chair of horror," my mother had done all the shopping. I had two pairs of jeans, one pair of dress pants, five shirts, four pairs of socks, a pair of dress shoes, and a pair of sneakers. That part of my day had been painless too.

CHAPTER 27

"TWO NINETY-FIVE FOR A BUCKET OF THIGHS—YOU CAN'T even cook 'em at home that cheap—and I didn't get any!" That's what Ginny Williams told me over the phone last night when I called to ask about the success of "Thigh Day" at Cossar's Fried Chicken.

More than likely, it would have never come to my attention had I not read about it on page two of last week's *Sawyerton Springs Sentinel.* There was a big picture of George, his wife, Betty Jo, and their three kids in front of the restaurant. Behind them, over the door, stretched a big banner that proclaimed: WE ARE OVERSTOCKED!

I suppose Thigh Day might not have been reported in most towns. Certainly the majority of newspapers would have overlooked the event, but Miss Edna Thigpen, the editor of the state's eighth oldest newspaper, feels an obligation to her readers. Until recently (when she discovered that the *Sentinel* actually was the state's eighth oldest newspaper), the *Sentinel's* official motto had been "All the News." That is still her goal.

Even though I left Sawyerton Springs years ago, I still subscribe to the *Sentinel*. It only costs nine dollars a year, and it allows me to share in the daily occurrences of the town in which I grew up.

How else would I know that the Genealogical Society had held its meeting last week at Christopher and Katherine Surek's house? According to the *Sentinel*, the Sureks were wonderful hosts, serving members and guests punch and pound cake from a beautifully decorated table.

Mr. and Mrs. Surek, natives of Zachery, Louisiana, now residing in Sawyerton Springs, also presented the program, which was a detailed account of the history of the house, known locally as the Jean Stimpson residence. A good time was had by all.

The article went on to compliment Mrs. Surek on restoring the flower beds "of which Jean was so proud" and listed the names of all the members, who incidentally answered the roll call by naming "favorite women in the Bible." Next month's program, I understand, will be presented by Lacy Bird Smith, who will speak on "What Happened to the Confederate Dead at Gettysburg."

The *Sentinel* has been owned and operated by Miss Edna since she took over for her father in 1948. She is pretty much the bottom line where editorial content is concerned. In fact, the only part of the paper she doesn't control is the weekly column, "What's On My Mind," written by her best friend and roommate, Miss Luna Myers.

Miss Edna and Miss Luna have lived together since they both turned sixty and it became apparent that neither would ever marry. Both are tall, thin, and have short, jet-black hair, which at a glance is quite obviously dyed. They are both eighty-three years old and despite their age show no signs of slowing down.

Miss Luna, in addition to her weekly column and occasional duties as a reporter, still works with the county health department and chairs several committees at the Grace Fellowship Baptist Church. Miss Edna, however, is a different story. The newspaper is her life. She writes the articles, takes the pictures, and sells the advertising. On Thursday evenings, she even stands over the boys from the high school shop class as they run her ancient printing press.

The *Sentinel* hits the streets early Friday morning and has usually been read by everyone in town by lunch. Week after week, Miss Edna provides Sawyerton Springs with something to talk about. Usually what they talk about are the mistakes they found in that week's edition.

No one really minds. "After all, she's eighty-three," they'll say. "Bless her heart."

Finding the mistakes has become a pastime for most of the townsfolk. Rather than mentioning the errors directly (that would be disrespectful to Miss Edna), most people simply slide them into their conversation. For instance, Billy Pat Williams might say to Kevin Perkin's son, "Hey, Judson! Great game the other night. I saw in the paper where you scored two *touchdogs!*" They'd both smile and go on their way.

Last December, the Christmas edition came out with PEACE OF EARTH! printed on the front page. Shortly thereafter, the sign on Roger Luker's real estate office read: THE PRICES WILL NEVER BE BETTER—GET YOUR PIECE OF EARTH NOW! The spelling was different, but everyone knew what he meant.

Miss Edna, in my estimation, also has a history of being overly dramatic in her choice of words. When I was fourteen, I was one of several boys caught rolling the yard of a teacher. We had gotten together one night and decided that Mrs. McEwen, of sixth period English, needed toilet paper in her yard. And in her trees. And on her house.

Suffice it to say we did a wonderful job, but we got caught and were forced by our parents, our principal, and Mrs. McEwen's husband, Bob, to clean up the mess. The next day, a picture of us doing so appeared on the *Sentinel's* front page—along with a caption that read: VANDALS ARRESTED AND PUNISHED!

This past week, however, Miss Edna finally took the cake. And if you wondered why Ginny Williams missed out on the thighs at Bubba's Fried Chicken, here is your answer.

It all started when Dr. Lee Peyton decided to have a small party at his office on Friday evening. It was to be a celebration of two years in family practice and only the people who owned businesses in town were asked to attend. The invitations, which were done in Old English script, stated simply: "You are cordially invited to attend an open house at the office of Dr. Lee Peyton between the hours of five-thirty and eight o'clock, Friday, the sixteenth of this month. Food and drink will be served."

All twenty-four invitations were mailed early in the week. No RSVP had been requested—it was simply assumed that everyone would show up. That's how things work in Sawyerton Springs. If you're asked to be somewhere, you go. It doesn't matter if it's a party or to help a neighbor fix a leaky septic tank. Of course, it's always more fun if it's a party.

On Thursday, Lee and his wife, Rebecca, spent the afternoon readying the office. It wasn't so much that Rebecca wanted to decorate; she just wanted certain things out of sight. "For gosh sakes, Lee," she said as she rolled her eyes, "people will be eating and drinking. They don't want to be staring at an exhibit of what happens to an ear when you don't wash it!"

Down also came the "Smoker's Lung" poster and the photographic enlargement of an ingrown toenail. Together they moved an examining table into the lobby. Lee began to cover it with a sheet, but one look from Rebecca told him he'd better get the tablecloth from home like she'd told him earlier.

The menu was set—pimento cheese sandwiches cut into small triangles, chicken salad sandwiches cut into small squares, and tuna fish on rye sandwiches cut into fingers. Mixed nuts, apple tarts, and vanilla wafers were also to be served. Rebecca had already made the sandwiches and stored them in the refrigerator. The nuts, tarts, and wafers, along with Cokes and coffee were to be picked up from Norman's Groceteria around three o'clock the next day.

Friday morning, Lee and Rebecca slept late. This being Lee's normal day off, the clinic wasn't open, and what with the party later that afternoon, they figured they needed the rest. In any case, neither of them so much as went outside until it was time to go by Norman's. So neither of them saw the *Sentinel*.

It wasn't until about ten minutes after five o'clock when Lee strolled outside the office. "I'm going to make sure the yard is clean," he said to his wife as the door shut behind him. Actually, he knew the yard was clean, but darn it, she was making him nervous. "Watch where you sit. Don't touch the apple tarts!"

Geez, Louise, he thought as he grabbed the paper on the way out, *this is just a little get-together. It's not like we're having the whole town for supper!* Lee chuckled as he broke the rubber band and opened the *Sentinel.*

Suddenly, his face went white. There on the front page, above the fold, was the invitation to the open house. His jaw dropped as he tried to comprehend what he was seeing. Evidently Miss Edna Thigpen of the *Sawyerton Springs Sentinel,* "The State's Eighth Oldest Newspaper," believing that everyone else got an invitation too, reprinted it verbatim. She even included a story about proper dress on such an occasion!

"Geez, Louise," Lee said as he dropped the paper and bolted for the door, "we *are* having the whole town for supper . . . and they're all going to be here in about five minutes!"

Actually, it took about thirty minutes for the town to get there . . . but the food was gone in five. About four hundred people actually showed up and all of them were hungry. Lee had already given Rebecca a sedative and was about to take one himself when he had an idea.

George. Yes, that might do it, he thought. George Cossar had told him yesterday that he and Betty Jo would be late to the party because he would be frying thighs. Anticipating an early rush the next morning, George was cooking in advance!

And so with one phone call, Thigh Day was cancelled and the party was saved. And no one beyond Lee and Rebecca or George and Betty Jo ever knew there was a problem . . . or who created it.

As for Miss Edna, she was never told what happened. Despite the fact that she reviewed the party and made derogatory comments about serving the dark meat of a chicken, neither Lee nor Rebecca ever said a word. George never got rattled or upset. In fact, none of them seemed to mind the trouble Miss Edna had caused.

"After all, she's eighty-three," they said. "Bless her heart."

CHAPTER 28

"A NINE-POUND HAM?" BILLY PAT WILLIAMS STARED INCREDulously at his wife, Ginny. "Are you telling me that that dog . . ." he said, pointing to his faithful companion, Barney, sprawled on the kitchen floor, ". . . that *that* fifty-pound dog ate a nine-pound ham?" Barney looked up and groaned.

Ginny said, "He's a fifty-nine-pound dog now."

"This isn't funny, Ginny," Billy Pat said. "How did it happen?"

"Well," Ginny answered, "I called Norman's to have a ham delivered. Evidently, I didn't hear the doorbell, because it was left on the back porch. The ham was wrapped, packaged, taped, and boxed. Barney tore a hole through the package and ate the ham through the hole—never even bothered to take it out of the box."

"That ham must have cost twenty dollars," Billy Pat said. "Was there anything left?"

"It was $36.50," Ginny replied, "and we've got a bone. You in the mood for soup?" She smiled. Barney groaned. Billy Pat cursed. "In any case," Ginny continued, "I guess we'd better call David."

As the only veterinarian in Foley and the surrounding area,

David Dykes worked most Saturdays, and this was no exception. David was currently occupied at his examination table. "This is one mean cat," he said to Paige, his assistant, as he prepared to sterilize a cut on the animal's tail. "This is Lamont, the Perkins's cat. This is a demon cat. The last time I treated this thing, he got loose and almost wrecked the place. Hold him tight."

Paige shifted Lamont to her left hand just as the phone rang. The cat seized the moment. In one fluid move, Lamont bit Paige on the arm, reached up with both paws, and grabbed for David's shoulder. From there, it was only a short hop to the highest point in the room, which was David's head.

Though he was scratched and bloody, David soon got things under control. He had been a vet for twenty years, and this was not the first time he had had a cat on his head. It was not even the first time he had had Lamont on his head, but David never got flustered. He was as cool as the center seed in a cucumber.

"By the way," Paige said as she bandaged her arm, "that was Ginny Williams on the phone. Their Dalmatian ate a ham, so they're bringing him in. She ought to be here in about twenty minutes."

"A ham," David said. "I'll bet Billy Pat hit the roof! So, is the dog—Barney, isn't it—sick?"

"I don't think so," Paige answered. "Ginny didn't say that he was."

The next several hours were business as usual for David. He vaccinated several dogs and cats, set a parakeet's broken wing, and super-glued the tail back on Jacob Perkins's lizard. He also ran his hands over Barney's hard stomach and calmed Ginny Williams's fears about intestinal ruptures, pork allergies, and swine flu.

David had already sent Paige home and was about to leave himself when the phone rang. "Dykes' Veterinary Clinic," he answered.

"Is this Dr. Dykes?" asked the caller with a frantic tone in his voice.

"Yes, it is," the veterinarian said. "Can I help you?"

"I hope so," the man replied. "I'm calling from a pay phone at a gas station. Rollins's Gas, the sign says."

"Yes," David said. "You're at Dick Rollins's place in Sawyerton Springs. I know where you are. What's wrong?"

"Are you a veterinarian?"

"Yes, I am. What's wrong?"

"You treat all kinds of animals and stuff like that?"

David was already tired, and he was beginning to get exasperated. "Look, when I answered the phone, I said 'Dykes' Veterinary Clinic.' My last name is Dykes, so I must be a veterinarian and this must be my clinic. Yes, I treat all kinds of animals and stuff like that. Now, tell me what's wrong."

David drove to Rollins's Gas Station mumbling to himself. The man had never told him what was wrong. "I shouldn't even be doing this," David said to himself. "I should be home right now."

It was curiosity more than anything that led David to the gas station. Over the phone, just before the man hung up, he had heard Dick yelling for help. David distinctly heard Dick say, "For God's sake, get this thing away from me."

When David pulled into the station yard, he noticed a plain panel truck with the back door open. There was no writing on the sides of the truck, and its only identifying feature was an Indiana license plate. Dick came from behind the truck and ran straight to the car. "David," he said, "have you got a gun?"

"Well, no," David answered nervously. "Not a real one. Why? What's wrong?"

Dick turned and headed to the pay phone. "I got to get a gun," he said.

David quickly got out of his car and followed Dick. He grabbed his arm and said, "Listen, I'm tired of nobody telling me what's wrong here. Now stop for a second and fill me in."

Dick stared blankly at David for a moment then said, "A man came in here thirty minutes ago and asked to use the water hose. He opened the back of the truck and the biggest dang rat I have ever seen in my life came running out. I was standing by the high-octane pump and that rat came over and punched me right in the chest. It knocked me into the drink machine. I think I broke a rib."

David paused. "A rat?" he asked.

"The biggest dang rat I have ever seen in my life," Dick said. "Punched me right in the chest."

David was of a mind to examine Dick. It was not often he was given the opportunity to treat a hallucinating patient. Just as he was about to talk soothingly to his friend, a man ran from the station.

The man appeared to be about fifty years of age, slightly overweight, and as red as a beet. As he hurried toward the two men, he kept glancing over his shoulder.

"You Dykes?" he asked breathlessly.

"Who are you?" David asked.

"Mike Jakubik," the man said without offering his hand. "I'm president of Mike's Sideshows from Indianapolis. We were meeting up with a carnival in Mobile when my main attraction went nuts. He practically tore up my truck. I almost had a wreck. I'm lucky I was able to pull into this service station."

"I know I'm thrilled," Dick muttered.

"Anyway," the man said as he started back toward the station, "I have him cornered in the restroom. I need you to get him back in the truck. Come with me."

David gathered up and loaded a tranquilizer pistol from the trunk of his car. As they walked toward the station, he asked Dick, "Just what are we dealing with here?"

"A rat," Dick said simply. "The biggest dang rat I ever saw in my life—punched me right in the chest."

As David peered through the semi-darkness of the mechanic's bay into the open door of the restroom, he wondered if Dick might be right. Maybe it was a rat. This Mike fellow had said he was from a carnival. Maybe this was a rat the size of a horse—a mount for Jimmy, the Two-Headed Jungle Boy, or something weird like that.

David was aggravated that Mike Jakubik hadn't told him any more than he had. And he had not seemed in the mood to help. Presently Mike was on the phone, which left David and Dick to hunt the unknown. David eased around an ancient Buick and brandished the tranquilizer gun like a cop on a late movie. Dick was about ten feet behind him.

David had never actually fired the pistol before. He had ordered it from a veterinary supply house in Columbus, Mississippi, several years before, and only three darts had been included in the $59.95 special. Now here in the quiet semi-darkness of the garage, listening intently to the ever-increasing beating of his own heart, David wished he had sprung for a suit of armor or a tank.

Suddenly, it was right in front of him. "Good Lord," David said sharply. The animal stood nearly as tall as David, and he appeared to be very angry. For a brief moment, the word *rat* did course through David's mind, but as the animal jumped over his head, he knew it was a kangaroo.

It was a boxing kangaroo apparently. When it jumped over David's head, it landed in front of Dick and punched him right in the chest. Again. When Dick yelled, David pulled the trigger and fired a dart into the commotion. Dick yelled again as the dart found its mark—the fleshy part of his left hip.

As he slumped toward the floor, losing consciousness quickly, Dick took a drunken swing at the kangaroo and missed. The kangaroo did not. It jumped into the air and—pow, pow, pow—punched Dick three more times.

The next dart David fired was successful. It clipped the angry animal just above the shoulder. Almost immediately, the kangaroo calmed down and was soon sleeping peacefully beside Dick on the floor.

"Thank God, you did it," Mike Jakubik said as he opened the door. He had been watching through the window. David had a third dart loaded and was tempted to use it on Mike, but he refrained. He helped the kangaroo back into the trailer and collected his fee.

As the panel truck drove away, Dick staggered toward David. "My chest hurts," he said. "What the heck was that thing?"

"That, my friend," David answered with a grin, "was the biggest dang rat I have ever seen."

CHAPTER 29

I͏T WAS THE LAST DAY OF SCHOOL—THE REALLY LAST DAY—I was a senior and would not be back the following year. First period was about to begin in Miss Wheeler's English class as I slumped at my desk. Kevin Perkins and Lee Peyton slumped at theirs. We were not slumping because we were depressed—we were slumping because we were seniors, and that was what we did.

"Good morning, class," Miss Wheeler said as she entered. "Sit up straight, please. Actually, I guess you don't have to." She smiled. "This is our last day together, and I've said that every morning for a year. It doesn't seem to have had any effect." We laughed.

Miss Wheeler was the favorite teacher at Sawyerton Springs High School. Most of the twenty-eight members of our graduating class had been third graders with Miss Wheeler. We caught up with her again in the seventh grade and were now ending our high school career with a lady who had become a part of our lives.

"I have seen most of you almost every day for the past ten years," she said. "I was just out of college when I began teaching third grade at the elementary school, and many of you were in my

first class. I was young and scared—so were you. In a way, I guess
we've grown up together.

"You are about to embark on a wonderful journey that will
most likely take you out of my life. Graduation is tonight. That is
not an ending but a beginning. Remember, there are great things in
store for you all."

At that point, I stopped listening. Miss Wheeler continued
talking in the same vein about things I did not want to hear. In
the months leading toward graduation, I had begun a steady climb
toward total confusion. I didn't have a plan for my life.

Everyone else seemed to know what they wanted to do. I, on
the other hand, was lost. Lee Peyton was going to be a doctor. Kevin
was going to be a builder. Sharon Holbert wanted to go to nursing school, and Steve Krotzer was determined to become a biolo-
gist. Roger Luker wanted into real estate, and Dickie Rollins didn't
care—he just wanted to make money.

I had already been accepted at Auburn University (I was set to
enter the pre-vet program in the fall), but my choice of college or
career held no magic for me. It was merely something to do.

I was more interested in what I could do to make someone
laugh. My choice of a major was even a part of that process. "I want
to be a veterinarian and a taxidermist," I'd tell people when they
asked. "Then—either way—you'll get your dog back."

Suddenly, I was snapped back into reality. Miss Wheeler was
calling my name. "Yes, ma'am?" I answered.

"Well," she said laughing, "you haven't paid much attention
all year long. There's no reason for you to begin now." The class
laughed. "Andy," she continued, "please stop by here after school
today."

"Uh-oh," Kevin said loud enough to start everyone giggling.
Miss Wheeler cut her eyes toward Kevin and said, "I just have a few
things to go over with you before the ceremonies tonight."

The bell rang, and as we walked out the door toward study hall,
Lee and Kevin fell in beside me. "What have you done now?" Lee
demanded. "You didn't fail a test, did you? Wheeler Dealer isn't

going to hold up your graduation, is she?"

"Do you think she knows about the flagpole?" Kevin asked.

"I hope not," I mumbled.

The Friday night before, Kevin, Lee, and I had taken fifty-two old tires from the dump behind Rollins's Gas Station and carried them to the base of the flagpole in front of the school. Then, taking turns, we climbed the pole fifty-two times—each time with a tire hanging on our heads—and deposited them over the top of the pole.

We did this until there was a vertical stack of tires forty feet high that totally covered the pole. It had taken us until almost daylight to finish, but the results had been worth the effort.

The tires remained around the flagpole for several days. A picture of the stack was on the front page of the *Sentinel*, and it was Wednesday afternoon before old Mr. Hawthorne, the school janitor, cut them off with a chain saw.

After study hall was Mrs. Shannon Smith and third period world history. I was fond of Mrs. Smith, but her course bored me into oblivion. I often wished I had been born two hundred years earlier so I wouldn't have had so much history to learn.

Fourth period: economics. Mr. Rodney Rosen. Raging Rodney Rosen. We almost stopped in the hall before entering the room to get down on our knees and thank God that we would not be seeing Raging Rodney again. For a year, we had listened to him scream (he never talked in a normal tone of voice) about politics.

Raging Rodney also talked in sayings—and he had a million of them. "Congratulations!" he yelled at us. "This is the first day of the rest of your life. Remember, there's no free lunch. What you get for free on this earth you can put in your eye, and it won't hurt."

He was screaming now. His face was red. "Listen for the sound of an oncoming train," he said. "Listen hard. If you don't hear trouble coming, it'll be on you in a New York minute." After an hour, the bell rang. It was only an extension of the ringing in my ears. So long, Mr. Rosen.

At lunch, Lee said, "She's gonna whup a zero on you for something. You ain't graduating tonight, Bud."

"She wouldn't," I said. "Would she?"

"I bet she found out about the cannon," Kevin said. He put his head on the table. "You're in for it, man."

Two months earlier, on the morning of April 1, it was discovered that the school cannon had been stolen. It was a Civil War cannon that weighed well in excess of one thousand pounds, and for the past thirty-eight years, it had been the only object on the front lawn of Sawyerton Springs High. There were no trees, no shrubs—just a huge lawn with a cannon on it. The cannon had been mounted on a concrete slab, which added to its bulk and weight.

The town was in an uproar. There was no evidence, save a big hole in the ground and a monstrous pile of dirt—the cannon was just flat-out gone. Paul Krupin, our principal, did an interview with the *Sentinel* and even appeared on the local news, Channel 4 from Dothan. "How," he said over and over, "does someone steal a cannon that, with its base, weighs around a ton? And where do you put it?"

The school board and city council organized searches and hired divers to check under bridges all over the county. No cannon. In fact, there were no clues at all until someone happened to notice four words in the classifieds of the *Sentinel*.

The four words were listed under "Miscellaneous" between the Hamilton's Shitzu puppies and Rick Carper's continuing search for a stainless steel bus jack. Four little words that had been appearing for several weeks *before* the cannon's disappearance. Only four words: *Look under the dirt.*

The cannon had never been stolen. A hole had been dug beside the cannon and the dirt had been piled on top. It was an illusion worthy of Houdini. We were very proud.

Fifth period was calculus. That was torture. I don't even want to think about it now.

Sixth period gym was over in a heartbeat. Coach Rainsberger had never been the most conscientious teacher, and that day was no different. He let us out early.

When the final bell rang and all the kids cleared the hallway, I went into Miss Wheeler's classroom. She closed the door. "What have I done?" I asked nervously.

"Nothing," she said smiling. "Calm down and take a seat." I did and she began to talk.

"I just want to tell you a story about a girl I knew. She was different from her friends. Her friends seemed so sure of themselves—about where they wanted to go in life and what they wanted to accomplish. This girl had hopes and dreams—and some fears—that were so deep inside her . . ." Miss Wheeler paused and wiped away a tear.

"To make a long story short," she went on, "this girl never accomplished the things she wanted because of the opinions and expectations of other people. She wanted to be a writer, to make people laugh and then cry and then laugh again. But her parents and friends said she should be happy for the opportunities she had. They told her to be normal." Miss Wheeler looked at me.

"So you became a teacher?" I asked. "Why?"

"I was scared," she said. "Scared of failing, scared of what others might think, just . . . scared. Please understand there is nothing wrong with teaching. It is a wonderful profession, but real misery is asking yourself 'what if' every day of your life.

"I asked you in here today to tell you that there is a reason you don't feel content with where you are going. I wanted to tell you that it is okay to be different. A person's difference can change the world but only if they gather the courage to use it. You are special, and by having the courage to stand up and be counted, you will inspire others to do the same."

I stared at her for a moment as a load lifted from my heart. "Thanks," I said. "Really. Thank you, I mean, a lot."

"No problem," she said. "Get on out of here. I'll see you tonight." I shook her hand and walked toward the hallway. "Andy," she said as I reached the door.

I turned around. "Ma'am?"

"I want you to carry two things with you as you leave. One: I am very proud of you. Two: I am giving you until your twentieth high school reunion to make things happen. After that, I am going to tell everyone in town about the flagpole and the cannon!" She smiled and hugged me. Then she pushed me through the door and into my life.

SUMMER
AGAIN

CHAPTER 30

IT IS LATE JUNE, AND SAWYERTON SPRINGS IS WELL INTO summer again. After calling several friends in and around town the past couple of weeks, I have come to the amazing conclusion that nothing of any note has occurred. This, of course, puts me in the awkward position of confessing to you, the reader, that there is no "bang" with which to end this book. You have stayed with me for a year. I promised you that the facts I related to you would not be boring. And here at last they are. In truth, I have nothing about which to write.

It was bound to happen sooner or later . . . nothing, I mean. That is the risk a scribe takes when he or she (and in this case, me) ties himself to a particular location—especially if that location happens to be Sawyerton Springs.

I must admit that I was tempted to simply make something up like real authors do, but since I am in this instance a historian of sorts, and you have come to expect the truth, anything less would be unfair. Besides, it would be too easy for you to catch me.

My challenge is in relating anything of interest with the information I received this month from my regular sources. It's tough to put several thousand words on paper based on the news that "it is hot." Seven different people gave me that same answer to my question about what was happening in town.

Actually, the heat is probably part of the reason I wasn't able to get a complete story from anyone. The people in Sawyerton Springs are generally a good-natured bunch, and for this past year, I think they put up with my invasion of their privacy quite well. But when temperatures exceed one hundred degrees for days on end, even the well mannered can become testy.

"Hot enough for you?" That's all I said to Miss Edna Thigpen yesterday afternoon when I got her on the phone. "No, Andy," she said, "I'd like to crank it up another hundred degrees so that my blood actually begins to boil!" (Whew! Sorry I asked, Miss Edna. I'll touch base with you some other time.)

Heat does that to people. Especially to the kind of people who are embarrassed by air conditioning. A prevailing opinion among some of the older residents seems to be, "My father got along without it, and it ain't no hotter now than it was then!" To them, a window unit is a visible sign of weakness.

It is fortunate then, I suppose, that most people in town do have air conditioning. As hot as it gets there, it would be a grouchy place without it.

As it is, tempers flared at the town council meeting last week. Kevin Perkins and Roger Luker almost got into it over the curfew controversy. "It was a dumb idea to begin with," Kevin said, "and three days of it is enough!"

Roger, still the town's only policeman, had instituted a curfew for kids younger than eighteen. He blew the fire whistle at ten o'clock sharp. This was done with the blessings of a town worried sick about their children—and all because of an article in the newspaper. Miss Luna Myers had written a piece in the *Sentinel* entitled: WILL YOUR BOY BE A CRIP OR A BLOOD? The subhead was "Gang Activity . . . Is It Headed Our Way?"

The immediate impact of the article was to make the town suspicious of its youth. Tom Henley, the owner of Henley's Hardware, refused to sell spray paint to Todd Rollins. "If your daddy really wants this to paint a porch swing," Tom told him, "he'll be more than happy to pick it up himself."

When Dick arrived at the store, Tom said, "I'm sorry, but that article said red was a gang color, and I didn't figure you'd want to take the chances with the life of your boy." Dick understood.

Quickly, the young people were on virtual probation. Was the youth choir from the Baptist church really taking rocks out of the churchyard to keep them from hitting the lawn mower, or were they collecting them to throw through someone's window? Who knew?

The curfew was in place before most people had discussed it, but soon cooler heads prevailed, and it was removed. The children in this town had never really done anything bad before, so what were they all upset about? "And besides," Kevin said before he sat down, "when the whistle blows at ten, it's waking everybody up!"

After telling me that it was hot, Foncie Bullard told me that everything was going well at Vacation Bible School. She, Melanie Martin, and Glenda Perkins were teaching the first, second, and third graders this year at Grace Fellowship Baptist Church.

For a week (in air conditioning), the ladies showed the children how to build churches out of Play-Dough and make potholders out of Popsicle sticks. They taught them songs like "Deep and Wide," "The B-I-B-L-E, Yes! That's the Book for Me," and "If You're Happy and You Know It, Clap Your Hands [clap, clap]."

Having been raised in a Catholic home, Foncie had not been aware until recently of the many variations on that particular song. There was "If You're Happy and You Know It, Stomp Your Feet [stomp, stomp]," "If You're Happy and You Know It, Say Amen [a-men]," and, of course, the ever popular "If You're Happy and You Know It, Do All Three [clap, clap; stomp, stomp; a-men]."

Foncie enjoyed story time most of all. It was a chance to listen to the children's comments about different Bible characters. On Thursday, she watched Glenda and Melanie skillfully act out the story of David and Goliath, after which Foncie asked the second graders if anyone knew the moral of the story. One of the boys did. "Duck," he said.

Melanie also enjoyed watching her own daughter, Missy, interact with the other first graders. Missy is an intelligent, self-assured little girl who is the spitting image of her mother—same hairstyle, same bright smile. She also has the same quick mind of her parents.

Last year, her father, Mike, inadvertently backed the car over the family dog. All the rest of that day, he and Melanie agonized over how to explain to Missy what had happened. "Honey," they finally told her, "Mullet has gone to be with God."

Missy had one question. "Well," she wanted to know, "what does God want with a dead dog?"

"I'm sorry," Norman Green said when I called. "There's really nothing going on. I hate you haven't got anything to write about. I'd go do something crazy for you myself if it weren't so dang hot."

Norman has been working in his garden at night to escape the heat. With a flashlight, he bends over and pulls weeds from around his tomatoes. This year Norman planted corn, peas, butter beans, cucumbers, okra, yellow squash, bell peppers, zucchini, and tomatoes. So did everyone else in town.

Growing up as I did in Sawyerton Springs, I thought for a while that it was actually a law that one had to have a garden. It was sort of strange, now that I think of it. We all planted the same things, we admired them in each other's backyards, then we gave it all to each other.

Every Sunday, the foyer at church looked like a roadside vegetable stand. Sacks of tomatoes, corn, cucumbers, and zucchini—especially zucchini. "We had more than we needed," my father would say to Mr. Rawls as he handed over a grocery sack full of the green squash. "Hope you can use them!"

Mr. Rawls would smile and say as how they certainly could as he admired the color, texture, and firmness of what he said was his favorite vegetable. Then he would give us a bag of tomatoes and okra, which believe it or not, just happened to be my dad's favorite.

Although the following week my father might give okra and

tomatoes to the Rawls and get zucchini in return, no one ever tired of this tradition. We gave each other so much that, by the time I turned eigthteen, I doubted whether I had ever eaten anything from our own garden.

We all enjoyed an ample amount of whatever we planted with one glaring exception. Watermelons. No one had any luck growing watermelons. Even though we all tried year after year, there seemed to be something about the soil in our area that precluded growing watermelons.

As a community, we longed to quit trying to force these melons to grow where they obviously did not want to, and every year, we determined to do just that—quit. But every year, the *Sentinel* would run a picture of someone from Foley or Dothan or somewhere else close by, and they would be holding a watermelon that weighed a thousand pounds or somewhere ridiculously close.

I cannot exaggerate the impact those pictures had on our town. "Look at this," someone would say. "I don't believe it! Why, it says right here that the man just threw some seeds out his kitchen window and got this monster for his efforts. Dad-blame-it! This didn't happen forty miles from here. If this moron (pronounced mo'- ron) can do this by accident, I know I can grow one. Look at the guy. He doesn't (pronounced dud-un) look like he has the sense to come in out of the rain!" And soon, the whole town would be planting watermelons again.

Summer after summer this went on until one year Haywood Perkins, Kevin's father, hit pay dirt. His garden was in a secluded area behind their house. Consequently, no one ever got a really good look at how things were coming along. Around town, word from Haywood was that he "just might have something this year in the watermelon department."

I'll always remember the look on the faces of the people at church that Sunday morning in July when Mr. Perkins drove up in a pickup truck loaded down with huge watermelons. "We had more than we needed," he said to the group gathered around his truck. "I hope you can use them." Then he walked inside.

Mr. Perkins never professed any great knowledge or secret formula. Neither had he sold his soul to the watermelon devil. He seemed to be as perplexed as everyone else . . . until the following year.

One July morning, about lunchtime, a man in a truck full of watermelons pulled up in front of Henley's Hardware. Several of the town's businessmen were standing out on the curb. "Excuse me," he said, "I came through here last year selling melons and found a guy who bought my whole load. I don't know his name, but I'd sure like to find him again." The men just looked at each other. The jig was up.

I'm quite sure that right now in Sawyerton Springs, as hot as it is, there is a boy working in his father's garden, because it will never be *his* garden until he has a boy of his own who is old enough to work in it.

As a teenager, I dug the soil, planted the seeds, pulled the weeds, and watered the plants. Then when my father had friends over, he would invite them to take a look at his garden! Astoundingly, the year I moved away from home, Dad decided that he was getting too old to have a garden. He was forty-two at the time.

As I close this last chapter of my hometown's activities, it occurs to me that maybe I did have something to write about after all. I am certain that it was not as thrilling as it might have been had I made it up, but I suppose that's the magic of this place . . . that it is *not* thrilling.

It is a place where the paper comes out once a week, and everyone already know what's in it. When the pastor speaks on Sunday morning, his congregation already knows what he will say. As the children bring home their report cards, the parents already know their grades. This is a place of character and love and memories. Good memories.

Finally, if you and I ever agree to dig further and participate in what the publishing industry will inevitably term "a sequel," please remember that if something unusual has happened in town, I will tell you. But if it is only hot, I will tell you that too. That is the risk a scribe takes when he or she (and in this case, me) ties himself to a particular location—especially if that location happens to be Sawyerton Springs.

The End

A Reader's Guide

for

Return to SAWYERTON SPRINGS

This Reader's Guide was created to facilitate a better understanding of your life by taking a deep breath, relaxing, and taking the time to find the humor and meaning in everyday life.

These questions may be used for group discussion or personal reflection. It is the author's hope that the reader's understanding of these principles and the inspirational life lessons in each chapter will lead to an extraordinary life and the desire to share these lessons with others.

GENERAL QUESTIONS

1. Why do you think Andy chose to include Miss Edna's newspaper, the *Sentinel*, in such an important role in the book? Do you think the book would have been the same without it? Explain your answer.

2. After reading *Return to Sawyerton Springs*, has your opinion or views on small towns changed? Have you or would you ever live in a small town? Why or why not?

3. Which lesson intertwined throughout this book resonates the most with you?

4. If you had to pick a favorite character from Sawyerton Springs, who would it be and why? What about that character draws you towards him or her?

5. What is your favorite chapter from *Return to Sawyerton Springs*? What about this chapter appeals to you?

CHAPTER 1

1. If you had to choose one capsule of time to carry with you for the rest of your life, what memory would you choose? What is it about this memory that is so important to you? What other memories still remain clear in your mind?

2. Why is it important to laugh and make your friends laugh? How does laughter affect your life? Can you recall a point in time when you laughed the hardest? How did it make you feel?

CHAPTER 2

1. If you saw someone stranded on the side of the road, would you stop to pick him/her up? Would it make a difference if it were a single person or a couple? Male vs. female? Why or why not? Why do stereotypes have an influence over your decision?

2. Why did Howard suddenly feel like he belonged in Sawyerton Springs? What made him change his mind?

CHAPTER 3

1. What was it about Andy's father, a.k.a. Brother Andrews, that made him so likable? What qualities did he possess? In what ways can your life benefit by applying these qualities to your persona?

2. Think back to the quote at the end of this chapter: "The measure of a person's worth is not in what he does—it's in what he is becoming" (Ch. 3, p. 33). What kind of affect does this quote have on you? What does it mean in your own words?

CHAPTER 4

1. "Well," he demanded, "you gonna throw it or not?" (Ch. 4, p. 35) Andy knew he shouldn't have thrown the tomato at the Vine and Olive Hotel. His gut instinct told him not to, yet he did it anyway. Do you think it is important to follow your instincts? How can you learn to be more aware of these intuitive messages?

2. "His powers of persuasion were of legendary proportions" (Ch. 4, p. 38). Why do you think Brian enjoys persuading others? Do you think he is right or wrong in his efforts to persuade others?

CHAPTER 5

1. "Both Dick and Joe blamed each other for the situation in which they found themselves" (Ch. 5, p. 42). Is it ever okay to place blame on someone? Have you ever been blamed for something you knew you didn't do intentionally? How did this make you feel?

2. Is it possible to turn any negative situation into a positive one? Where does perspective play a part?

3. Why did Andy choose to leave the story hanging at the end? What

do you think happened? Do you think Dick and Joe were finally able to forgive one another? Why is forgiveness so important?

CHAPTER 6

1. Why is it dangerous to harbor or manifest negative thoughts towards your relationships? How does open communication help eliminate this? By harboring negative thoughts, are you sabotaging yourself?

2. Ginny's mood automatically changed once she started thinking about the good qualities in Billy Pat. How can a grateful heart contribute to your happiness? Do you think it's possible to be happy whenever you choose? Why or why not?

CHAPTER 7

1. Why do we get the urge or feel the need to impress others—even if we know what we are doing is wrong? Is this need to impress part of the natural human condition? Do you think this contributes to how we learn and gain wisdom?

2. "For thousands of years, *chicken* has topped the list of the words most likely to provoke action from a boy" (Ch. 7, p. 54). Are there certain ways your friends know how to provoke you? How can you condition yourself to ignore words of provocation?

3. When you were a kid, was there someone your parents warned you not to hang around with? Were they right in warning you? Did you hang out with that person anyway? Why or why not?

CHAPTER 8

1. "To my thinking, 'a job like that' didn't seem half bad" (Ch. 8, p. 66). At what age did you start thinking about your future occupation? How much has your vision changed? Why is it important to have ambitions at an early age?

2. Why do you think Andy and his friends refused to believe the carnival games were rigged? Can you recall a time when you had to learn or experience something for yourself?

CHAPTER 9

1. What kind of community do you live in? A large city? A small town? What are some of its characteristics? How do they compare to Sawyerton Springs?

2. If you were given $10, how might you make it multiply? List 10 ideas that come to mind.

3. "Whether we think we can or we think we can't...either way we're right!" (Ch. 9, p. 74) Do you agree with this statement? Why or why not?

CHAPTER 10

1. Why do you think Roger felt "compelled to announce his name and business every time he shook" (Ch. 10, p. 76) someone's (including people he knew very well) hand? Have you ever met someone who did the same thing?

2. How do you think the town of Sawyerton Springs would have been affected had the deal to build a golf course went through? Was Roger wrong in wanting to make "the big deal"? (Ch. 10, p.

77) After all, he'd been waiting his entire life. Would you have been able to turn down that deal?

3. In this chapter, Andy describes Roger and Carol as having completely different personalities. Do you think this benefited their marriage? Why or why not?

Chapter 11

1. At what age did you want to be treated like an adult? Why do you think children want to be treated like an adult at such a young age?

2. In this chapter, Andy talks about one of life's ugly metaphors. "Just when the going was easy—just when everything was downhill—we had to go up the other side" (Ch. 11, p. 83). Have you experienced this metaphor in your own life? Discuss events from your life that remind you of this "ugly metaphor." Why is this metaphor such an important part of life? How can it be viewed as a positive part of life?

Chapter 12

1. Michael Ted Williams had an obsession with Elvis. Do you think it is possible to have "healthy" obsessions? How did Michael Ted use his obsession with Elvis in a positive way?

2. Andy describes Michael Ted as "a great old guy who provided us with laughter even after passing" (Ch. 12, p. 93). Why is laughter so important, not just to you, but also to other people around you? How can laughter affect one's day? Do you think laughter can extend your life?

3. Why do you think Michael Ted was so prepared for "the end"?

Do you think this preparation made it easier for Michael to let go of life?

Chapter 13

1. Did your parents ever scare you as a child? Why do you think we are so easily scared as children? Do you think the fear goes away as we become more mature? Is this based on our experiences? Explain your answer.

2. Why do you think people don't like other people to know they are scared? What is it about fear that makes someone seem weak? Do you think fear makes a person weak? Why or why not?

Chapter 14

1. "In a town like Sawyerton Springs, all the emergency services operate on a volunteer basis" (Ch. 14, p. 102). Do you think this would ever be possible in a large city? Why do you think the entire town is able to work together so well?

2. If you were put in the same situation as Kevin and found out you technically owned the entire town, how would you have handled the situation? Would greed have gotten in the way of your decision? Why do you think Kevin chose not to take advantage of the situation? Why is it so hard for humans to do the right thing?

3. Towards the end of this chapter, Kevin says to Olive, "We'll get it done tomorrow, Olive, and don't worry about where the money is coming from. I don't think it'll cost anything" (Ch. 14, p. 106). His hopes were that "someone would be of a mind to help Glenda [his wife] one day if something happened to him" (Ch. 14, p. 106). Do you believe in the idea that what goes around comes around?

CHAPTER 15

1. Why is it important to have "gratefulness in our hearts"? (Ch. 15, p. 108) How can gratefulness in your heart contribute to a better life? List 10 things that you are grateful for.

2. In this chapter, Wade is seen as having a very negative attitude towards life and is viewed as someone you don't want to be around. How can this negative attitude affect your relationships? Do you think a positive person and someone you enjoy being around gets more opportunities in life? Is the opposite true for someone like Wade? Explain your answer.

3. Is there something in your life that is preoccupying your mind and not allowing you to see the big picture? What does the "big picture" mean to you?

CHAPTER 16

1. Why did the town decide not to confront Rick and Sue about the "bad soup"? How might Rick and Sue have reacted had the town confronted them?

2. At the end of the chapter, Dick and Billy Pat realized Rick's soup was causing the town to get sick. How might you have reacted when Rick said, "I'm going to eat the last of our chicken soup"? (Ch. 16, p. 121) Would you have let him?

CHAPTER 17

1. What is it that causes a child to feel so different than his or her parents? At what age did this change for you?

2. Can you remember the first time your parents let you stay at

home alone? How did this make you feel? Do you believe that every person has a sense of self-independence instilled within him or her from the time they are born?

3. Why did Andy get so scared all of a sudden once he reached his house after walking home from church? What was different this time?

CHAPTER 18

1. Dave Winck "is known around town as a person who will do exactly as he is asked. *Exactly*" (Ch. 18, p. 131). Have you ever known someone like Dave? Why do you think Dave is the way he is?

2. Do you think the ping-pong giveaway idea would have been more successful in a larger town? Why or why not? Do you think the town would have been as eager and frantic had the Ping-Pong balls been dropped once the parade had ended?

CHAPTER 19

1. Does it make it right that Kevin ignored Glenda's feelings about him leaving for the week just because the trip was considered tradition? How could Kevin have handled the situation differently?

2. How could the other guys on the cabin trip (Kevin, Joe, Dick, and Roger) learn from Billy Pat in his decision to stay home and help Ginny first before having fun with the guys?

3. "Jerry has a reputation as a tough customer...the man takes his job seriously. He'd give me a ticket in a heartbeat" (Ch. 19, p. 137). Have you ever been in a job situation where you were able

to give a friend a discount or something for free? How did you handle the situation? Did your friend or family member attempt to guilt you into giving them a discount or freebie? How did this make you feel?

CHAPTER 20

1. Why is it so easy to place blame on someone else instead of accepting responsibility for your own actions?

2. Think of a situation when you were angry with someone. How did you attempt to calm down? Can this way of calming yourself be successful in other situations or with other emotions?

3. Why was the five-year-old girl able to calm the entire church down in the midst of the storm? Had it been an adult singing, do you think he or she would have had the same effect? Why or why not?

CHAPTER 21

1. Billy Pat Williams gets a lot of jokes thrown his way. In fact, the entire town is constantly making jokes towards one another. Why do you think the people in a small town like Sawyerton Springs tell so many jokes? How is the relationship between the town members different than that of a big town?

2. In the middle of the night, Billy Pat was instructed to break up a dogfight. If you were faced with the same situation, would you have had the guts to break up the fight? How would you have handled the situation?

Chapter 22

1. Do you remember your first love? How did he/she make you feel? What sort of things did you do to impress him or her? How often did those things actually work?

2. Andy takes advantage of a situation by convincing Sharon, the girl he loves, that he is dying so she'll like him back. Ultimately, to Andy's surprise, Sharon finds out. Have you ever taken advantage of a situation hoping for a positive result, but the final outcome ends up worse than you had anticipated?

3. Why do you think Sharon took so long to finally tell Andy she always "kinda" liked him? Why do you think they never ended up with each other even though they both shared the same feelings?

Chapter 23

1. Have you ever thought you had a great idea, but chose to sabotage yourself by thinking that it wasn't that good and would probably never work out? Are you letting yourself get in the way of being someone great? What steps can you take to avoid this self-sabotage? Remember, "Everybody thought Einstein was a nut case, too!" (Ch. 23, p. 166)

2. Can you recall a time when you had to be the bigger person? How did you react to the situation? Did you want to retaliate as Norman did or did you handle the situation differently? Explain your answer.

Chapter 24

1. Can you remember your favorite teacher? What do you remember about this teacher? What qualities made you like him or

her so much?

2. Do you have a favorite memory from school? Which emotions do you feel when you think about that memory?

3. Recall the quote, "Remember, to take advantage is to invite trouble" (Ch. 24, p. 175). Have you ever taken advantage of someone because you knew you could get away with it? In what way does this invite trouble?

CHAPTER 25

1. How can gossip lead to rumors? Have you ever been a victim of a rumor that started with gossip? How did this make you feel?

2. Why was Billy Pat more concerned with what he was wearing than with finding out what was hiding behind Miss Edna and Miss Luna's couch? Why do we care so much about what other people think? Should your image really matter? Explain your answer.

CHAPTER 26

1. Are there certain things that you remember doing as a child with your parents that you disliked? Do you still dislike these things? Why or why not?

CHAPTER 27

1. Do you think Miss Edna's newspaper, the *Sentinel*, helped unite the town? How might the town and the relationships between everyone be different without the *Sentinel*? Also, did it help that she was both dramatic and brutally honest?

2. "That's how things work in Sawyerton Springs. If you're asked to

be somewhere, you go" (Ch. 27, p. 192). Why do you think there is such a strong bond of trust among residents in the town of Sawyerton Springs? If one person in the town weren't as trustworthy as the rest, how do you think the town might be affected?

3. Because of a misprint by Miss Edna in the *Sentinel*, the entire town showed up for the open house at the office of Dr. Lee Peyton. "In fact, none of them seemed to mind the trouble Miss Edna had caused" (Ch. 27, p. 194). How would you have handled this situation had you been in Lee and Rebecca's shoes? Would you have been as patient with Miss Edna? Explain your answer.

Chapter 28

1. Andy describes David Dykes, the veterinarian, as being very patient. He says, "He was as cool as the center seed in a cucumber" (Ch. 28, p. 196). Is it difficult for you to be patient? Why is patience so important in everyday life? How can patience contribute to your happiness and well-being?

2. If you were faced with the same situation as David Dykes regarding the "giant rat," would you have had the confidence to go in after it?

Chapter 29

1. Did you have a plan for your life upon graduating from high school? Can you remember your last day? How did you feel? Nervous? Excited? Prepared?

2. Why is it so important not to let the opinions and expectations of others affect you? What kind of affect can these opinions and expectations of other people have on your life?

3. Reflect on the quote, "A person's difference can change the world, but only if they gather the courage to use it" (Ch. 29, p. 205). What does this quote mean to you? How can you apply it to your life?

CHAPTER 30

1. Why do you think Andy chose to end the book the way he did? Did his honesty make it more authentic?

ACKNOWLEDGMENTS

I AM BLESSED TO BE SURROUNDED BY FRIENDS AND FAMILY WHO have become a team of which I am thrilled to be a part. If I can ever be perceived as a person who makes good and informed choices, it is only because of my reliance on these people's wise counsel. Thank you all for your presence in my life.

. . . To Polly, my wife and best friend. You are beautiful, smart, and witty . . . after twenty years it is still a great combination.

. . . to Austin and Adam, our boys. You bring me joy and perspective. I never knew I could love so much.

. . . to Robert D. Smith, my personal manager and champion. After twenty-eight years together, you still amaze me every day.

. . . to Scott Jeffrey, the Bear Bryant of "life coaches."

. . . to Duane Ward and the whole incredible gang at Premiere Speaker's Bureau: You are not just partners—you are friends.

. . . to Mark Victor Hansen, the publisher; Patti Coffey and Gail Kingsbury from Hansen House Publishing; and Reid Tracy and Louise L. Hay from Hay House.

. . . to Sandi Dorff, Paula Tebbe, and Susie White, who direct the daily parts of my life. Without the effort, prayer, and attention to detail of these three ladies, my own efforts would not come to nearly so much.

. . . to Jared McDaniel, for his sense of humor and artistic ability.

. . . to Nicholas Francis for his Web mastery.

. . . to Nate Bailey for his organizational skills, happy demeanor, and "never say die" attitude.

. . . to Kevin Burr for his insight into the town of Sawyerton Springs and for creating the Reader's Guide. Your keen understanding of the purpose of this book is greatly appreciated.

. . . to Katrina and Jerry Anderson, Don Brindley, Sunny Brownlee, Foncie and Joe Bullard, Brent Burns, Myrth and Cliff Callaway, Gloria and Bill Gaither, Gloria and Martin Gonzalez, Lynn and Mike Jakubik, Patsy Jones, Karen and Alan McBride, Liz and Bob McEwen, Edna McLoyd, Mary and Jim Pace, Glenda and Kevin Perkins, Brenda and Todd Rainsberger, Kathy and Dick Rollins, Shannon and John D. Smith, Claudia and Pat Simpson, Jean and Sandy Stimpson, Dr. Christopher Surek, Maryann and Jerry Tyler, Wade, Pat, Joey, and Elizabeth Ward, Mary Ann and Dave Winck, and Kathy and Mike Wooley. Your influence in my life is undeniable, and your example is very much appreciated.

The
NOTICER

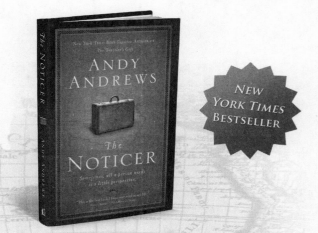

NEW YORK TIMES BESTSELLER

*Sometimes, all a person needs
is a little perspective.*

YOUR CHANCE TO REGROUP, TAKE A BREATH,
AND BEGIN YOUR LIFE AGAIN AWAITS IN THE
SIMPLE WISDOM AND HEARTWARMING STORY OF
A MAN NAMED JONES.

❧

This is the best book I have ever read in my life."

—NANCY LOPEZ,
LPGA Hall of Fame Golfer

THE
BUTTERFLY
EFFECT

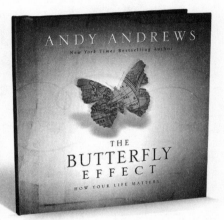

HOW YOUR LIFE MATTERS

*"Every single thing you do matters.
You have been created as one of a kind. You have been
created in order to make a difference. You have within you
the power to change the world."*

ANDY ANDREWS

Also by
ANDY ANDREWS

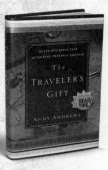

THE TRAVELER'S GIFT

This unique narrative is a blend of entertaining fiction, allegory, and inspiration. Master storyteller Andy Andrews gives us a front row seat for one man's journey of a lifetime. David Ponder has lost his job and with it, the will to live. Then something incredible happens. He is supernaturally selected to travel through time and gets the amazing opportunity to visit some of history's most remarkable people. There's Abraham Lincoln, King Solomon, and Anne Frank, among others. Each visit yields a distinct Decision for Success that will one day impact the entire world. On this journey, David Ponder is changed forever. You will be too.

ISBN: 0-7852-6428-0

THE LOST CHOICE

In *The Lost Choice*, *New York Times* bestselling author Andy Andrews brilliantly weaves a suspenseful tale of intrigue, inspiration, and enlightenment to offer readers a stunning glimpse into the power of their own actions. He provides clear, guiding principles for rediscovering our own "lost choices," and proves that everything we do—and don't do—affects not only our own lives, but also the lives of generations to come. In this unforgettable work, Andrews offers an inspiring, suspenseful tale of empowerment, connection, consequence, and purpose.

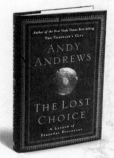

ISBN 0-7852-6139-7

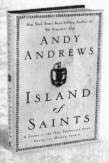

ISLAND OF SAINTS

Set in a period of worldwide turmoil and social resentment, *Island of Saints* offers a startlingly simple yet profoundly wise solution for healing the world. Blending his unique style of historical accuracy with unparalleled storytelling, *New York Times* bestselling author Andy Andrews illuminates a timeless truth taught by saints and sages for millennia.

In the spirit of *The Traveler's Gift* and *The Lost Choice*, Andrews brilliantly delivers a tale of war, faith, and, ultimately . . . forgiveness.

ISBN 0-7852-6140-0

THE TRAVELER'S GIFT TREASURY

The Traveler's Gift: It's the book that moved millions. In the tradition of bestselling books by Og Mandino, Andy Andrews' blend of fiction and allegory will inspire you to find true and lasting success in your life.

The Traveler's Gift Journal: The perfect companion to *The Traveler's Gift*, this journal gives you the opportunity to record your own experiences as you personally take hold of each of the seven decisions.

The Young Traveler's Gift: Adapted from the *New York Times* bestseller *The Traveler's Gift*, this book will provide young people with the wisdom needed to make powerfully sound decisions in today's turbulent world.

Timeless Wisdom from the Traveler (9 CDs): Join Andy Andrews for an in-depth analysis of the lessons revealed in his modern classic, *The Traveler's Gift*.

The Seven Decisions PBS Special (2CD Set): Millions were moved to life-changing action with this groundbreaking two-hour PBS special in which Andrews shares new insight into the powerful principles conveyed in his *New York Times* best-selling sensation *The Traveler's Gift*.

The Seven Decisions PBS Special (DVD): In this riveting, thought-provoking and often very funny live performance, Andy Andrews proves that everything you do matters, not just for you and your family—but for generations to come.

The Seven DECISIONS PERPETUAL CALENDAR

Put what you've learned into life-changing actions with **The Seven Decisions Perpetual Calendar.** The calendar lays the foundation to your success of incorporating The Seven Decisions into your daily way of thinking and living. When you read The Seven Decisions as laid out in the *New York Times* best-seller *The Traveler's Gift*, and combine those principles with the tools offered through these calendar formats, you will be able to develop the habits that will turn your goals and dreams into daily realities!

Andy Andrews' Seven Decisions Perpetual Calendar is offered as a
FREE DOWNLOAD online at AndyAndrews.com/Calendar

For this, and other exciting, life-changing resources, visit

ANDYANDREWS.com

Contact Hansen House Publishing

P.O. Box 7665
Newport Beach, CA 92658
www.HansenHousePublishing.com